Transforming My Attitude Through Gratitude

TRANSFORMING
MY ATTITUDE
Through
GRATITUDE

DR. RHONDA AUSTELL JAUDON

XULON PRESS

Xulon Press
2301 Lucien Way #415
Maitland, FL 32751
407.339.4217

www.xulonpress.com

Printed in the United States of America

Paperback ISBN-13: 978-1-6628-3906-1
Ebook ISBN-13: 978-1-6628-3907-8

Introduction:

The Evolution of the Book

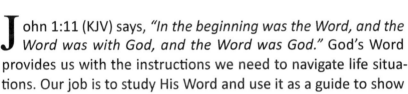

J ohn 1:11 (KJV) says, *"In the beginning was the Word, and the Word was with God, and the Word was God."* God's Word provides us with the instructions we need to navigate life situations. Our job is to study His Word and use it as a guide to show us how to live an abundant life full of his love, grace, and mercy. It is through His Word that we can find purpose while we are yet here on Earth.

The Word declares, *"I have given them thy Word; and the world hath hated them, because they are not of the world, even as I am not of the world. I pray not that thou shouldest take them out of the world, but that thou shouldest keep them from the evil"* John 17:11, (NIV).

Thank You, God, for covering me amid an evil society. *"To the only wise God be glory forever through Jesus Christ! Amen"* (Rom. 16:27, NIV).

It is His Word that shaped my attitude, faith, obedience, and dedication to walking with God in all seasons, even amid the worldwide pandemic that we are experiencing. COVID-19 runs rampant in this world, claiming many innocent lives with no discrimination. Romans 8:28 (KJV) says, *"And we know that all things work together for good to those who love God, to those who are the called according to His purpose."*

As such, through the unction of the Holy Spirit, I made it my mission to turn something evil into something good. The turmoil that the world was experiencing pushed me closer and closer to God and His Word. I sought after Him with all my heart, soul, and mind. As I studied the Word of God, my passion for journaling grew deeper and deeper. I found it confirming to get my thoughts on paper as a reminder of the goodness of God. While journaling throughout the pandemic, the spirit of God revealed to me this would be a tool for drafting an inspirational book to encourage the body of Christ. While I trusted the Lord, I wasn't quite sure how journaling could manifest itself into a book. Needless to say, I put the thought on the shelf and waited for God to speak.

God's Word reminds us that, *"To everything there is a season, and a time to every purpose under the heaven"* (Eccles. 3:1, KJV).

Be encouraged saints when God puts something in your heart to do, He will provide us with all the tools and resources needed to be successful.

Ephesians 2:10 (NASB) reveals that, *"We are God's workmanship, created in Christ Jesus for good works, which God prepared beforehand that we should walk in them."*

Low and behold, little did I know that the timing for drafting my book was at hand. On the last day of August 2021, I completed journaling my thoughts in a study of Proverbs. At the culmination of the study, I received a text from Evangelist Ella Brown that said, "Hello, my Sister-in-Christ. I would like to ask you to go on a journey with me in the month of September writing a gratitude journal. Gratitude is a deep feeling of appreciation for the people, circumstances, and material possessions in our life. It is one of the most powerful feelings God has given us. Gratitude is the greatest joy and meaning for our life. In September, write three things in your journal for which you are grateful. You can show people that you are grateful by sending an email, card, letter, and also praying for someone. It will shift our perspective in every area of our lives. I am grateful for you being in my life. Amen."

While I knew in my heart that this was a beneficial task to participate in, I felt that I didn't have enough time to give the task credence. So, I responded to her by text, "Good morning, Ella, I hope all is well. During September, I will be starting an inductive study: Walking with God in Every Season. Looking forward to your participation. See you in church. Love you!" Notice, I didn't say no to the gratitude journaling, but I didn't say yes. My unspoken message was, "I don't have the time to take on one more thing in my life. I will do this at a later time but not in September."

God is the great orchestrator of our lives, and we must learn to trust His plan. Little did I know, I was not in control of my destiny. Jeremiah 29:11 (KJV) states, *"For I know the thoughts that I think toward you, says the Lord, thoughts of peace and not of evil, to give you a future and a hope."*

On Sunday morning, August 29, 2021, I was permitted to deliver the message for the 11:00 service, "Walk by Faith and Not By Sight: Do You Trust Him." At the end of the service, Evangelist Ella Brown shared with the body of Christ about taking part in the gratitude journaling for September. While I listened with a spirit of humility, my mind was resolute that the timing for doing this was not right for me. The next morning when I woke, I went into the study for prayer, meditation, and studying the Word of God. During my silent time with God, the Holy Spirit spoke to me, telling me that I will take part in the gratitude journaling in September. I hastened to respond to the calling. My whole being could not say yes quickly enough. When God speaks, you will listen. I began to prepare for my gratitude experience.

I still did not know where this journey was leading me. Nevertheless, after the third day of journaling, the spirit of God spoke to me declaring that I share my thoughts with others through a book. In each journal entry, I was instructed to use *God names* to express my deepest *gratitude* for all His many blessings. This was the beginning of my journey. To God be the glory for all He has done.

While reading my journal of gratitude, put yourself, friends, and loved ones in your thoughts and begin to reflect on how much you love and appreciate God. The purpose of this book is designed to encourage the body of Christ to be grateful for the things that God has given you. Make it a point each day to look for all the blessings that are bestowed upon you, exalting God in all things.

Psalms 145:1-3 (NIV) says, *"I will exalt You, my God the King; I will praise Your name forever and ever. Every day I will praise You and extol Your name forever and ever."* Let the journey begin with day 1 as I share with you how grateful I am unto God.

Getting Started With Your Journal of Gratitude

1. Go before God daily in prayer thanking Him and seek Him daily for guidance and instructions.
2. Invite the Holy Spirit to lead and guide you through the process of journaling. Make sure your thoughts are reflective and intentional.
3. Find scriptures that are relevant to your thoughts as you record various things for which you are thankful.
4. Meditate on God's Word day and night and watch it transform your thinking and being. When we allow God's Word to move mightily in our lives, it shapes the very essence of our being.
5. Purchase a journal or create an electronic journal to record your feelings of gratitude.
6. Each day you read a journal entry from this book, reflect on the goodness of God. Then write three things in your journal for which you are grateful.
7. Be sure to record the day and date of each journal entry. Although optional, you may want to write the actual time of each journal entry.
8. Make it your mission to strategically bless someone and spread the joy. The act of blessing others creates a healthy, enthusiastic, and positive outlook on life. It is a feel-good drug that only comes from heartfelt giving unto others. In short, God is pleased when we are a blessing to others.
9. Invite others to join in on this crusade of gratefulness. We spend too much of our time complaining and wadding in self-pity. It is time for us to get up, take charge of our life, and give God the praise, honor, and glory He deserves.

Dedication

T his book is dedicated to my husband, Robert Jaudon, who supports me in all things. To my mother, Fannie Austell, who empowered me during my beginnings to know my self-worth and reach for the stars. To Evangelist Ella Brown, who is an inspiration and a hero in my life. Her faith and obedience to God inspire me to be my personal best in my relationship with the only wise God that can keep me from falling. Most of all, I honor the Holy Trinity for leading and guiding me through the process of expressing my thoughts of gratitude to God under His God names.

Contents

———————✳———————

Day 1

Wednesday, September 1, 2021

The Holy Trinity: Working Things Out For My Good

Entry One

Thank You, God, The Father, for Your love, mercy, and grace. If it had not been for Your love, I don't know where I would be at this point in my life. I reverence You, oh God, and thank you for health, peace, love, and strength. You have given me peace in my spirit that is incomprehensible. There was a time in my life when I was anxious about the things of tomorrow; I thank you for the shift in my thinking for I no longer am concerned about tomorrow because I know You hold tomorrow. If my faith is lacking in any department of my life, put me in a position to hear your word and walk in obedience. I give You praise and honor for using me as a vessel to serve you by serving your people. It is such a joyous feeling to have a relationship with you and know that your blessings and mercies are new and fresh each day.

Your Word declares, *"The Lord is good to all, and His tender mercies are over all in His works"* (Ps. 145:9, KJV).

You love me so much that You were willing to give up Your only begotten Son to become a substitutionary lamb for my sins; the One who is holy, blameless, and sinless. I thank You, God, for seeing the best in me, even when I don't deserve it; You look beyond my faults and see my needs. You are an awesome God and I reverence You in Your infinite Glory. I thank You for filling my heart with thanksgiving and praise for the countless blessings that You so freely give unto me. Your generosity to an undeserving saint like me overflows with gratitude. Today and forevermore, I will honor and meditate on the splendor of Your majesty and the extraordinary works that You have performed in my life and the lives of Your people. I honor Your greatness, Your holiness, and Your righteousness that gives me the strength to persevere until the end of times.

My God, My Father, *"Teach me to do Your will, for You are my God; Your Spirit is good. Lead me in the land of uprightness"* (Ps. 143:10, NKJV).

I am grateful that you took the time to cast Your Spirit upon me, teaching and leading me to live a righteous life, holy and acceptable in your sight. It is an honor to serve a covenant God who does not break promises. Everything that You have ever said in Your Word is true with a foundation that cannot be shaken. Your Son, Jesus, taught your Word in the flesh and He said, *"The scriptures cannot be altered"* (John 10:35, NIV).

Without a doubt, I know that your peace and blessings are upon me and everything I need can be found in You. I rest in the assurance that Your Word will always remain the same so I can walk with boldness and confidence in who I am in Christ Jesus.

1 Peter 2:9 (NIV) tells us, *"But you are not like that, for you are a chosen people. You are royal priests, a holy nation, God's very own possession. As a result, you can show others the goodness of God, for he called you out of the darkness into his wonderful light."*

Entry Two

I am so thankful to God, the Son, Jesus Christ. With much gratitude to You for being my role model of what it means to be obedient to the will of God, Your Father. The Word of God declares that, *"God so loved the world, that he gave his only begotten Son, that whosoever believeth in him should not perish, but have everlasting life"* (John 3:16, KJV).

It is through Your death, burial, and resurrection that I have the gift of salvation. Through Your redeeming blood, I am cleansed of my sins. Isaiah 53:5 (NIV) reveals, *"But he was wounded for our transgressions, he was bruised for our iniquities: the chastisement of our peace was upon him; and with his stripes we are healed."*

When I was born into this world, I had a death sentence hanging over my head. Satan was the hitman hired to kill, destroy, and devour me with a mission to send me straight to hell. I am grateful to You, Jesus, for stepping in with humility, authority, and victory. You reached out and grabbed sin and death and took it to the cross, releasing me from Satan's strongholds, chains, and bondage that were designed to keep me down. You are exalted for bringing me out of the shadow of death and destroying the bands of sin that shackled me from enjoying the richness of your glory. Romans 8:2 says, *"For the law of the Spirit of life has set you free in Christ Jesus from the law of sin and death."*

There is a saying that we can make a payment to buy a slave as a servant; But no price can be paid for salvation. This can only be granted through Jesus Christ, for the shedding of His blood gave us life when sin attempted to give us death. When Jesus and God consulted with each other, they didn't bring forth salvation so that we could go merely to heaven, it also transferred us to leave the kingdom of darkness to receive the kingdom of light. I am grateful that I am adopted in Christ, heir of my heavenly Father who grants me access to every spiritual blessing.

Jesus, I thank you for being a perfect model for how to live a righteous life; help me keep my heart, mind, and focus coordinated with You. I look not to mankind for direction but to you for guidance and spiritual leadership in my life. I surrender to You, all that I am, all that I have, and all that I hope to be. Hallelujah and glory to your name for you are worthy of the praise.

Thank You for Your healing blood and for bridging the gap between God and me. You are a wonderful Savior, and if I say it a trillion times, it will still not be enough.

Entry Three

Thank You, God, the Holy Spirit, for dwelling inside of me, enabling me to live a righteous and faithful life. Through Your power, I am saved, filled, sealed, and sanctified. Thank You for revealing God's thoughts, teaching, and guiding me into all truths, including the knowledge of what is to come. When I'm weak, You intercede on my behalf, strengthening me to persevere to see what the end will be.

While I live in an unholy world, God sent You, the Holy Spirit, to oversee me, to help me live a godly life that is reflective of His character. The day I became a child of God, I was put in a heavenly envelope, name printed in gold, sealed with the precious blood of Jesus, and guaranteed delivery to live with God forever by endowing it with the Holy Spirit.

2 Corinthians 1:22 (NIV), *"And he has identified us as his own by placing the Holy Spirit in our hearts as the first installment that guarantees everything, he has promised us."*

I thank you, Holy Spirit, for being forever present in my life, my advocate that was sent by the Father to teach, lead, and guide me. You are a blessing to me in so many ways in that you open my eyes, giving me the wisdom to see things from a spiritual view, crucifying my worldly perception of things. As I read God's Word, you are there to help me interpret the true message being conveyed, giving me the understanding to know the difference. You are eternal; You help me recognize the glory of God and enable me to know how to call on Jesus. I am grateful for Your role in my life and the gifts of the Spirit (i.e. wisdom, understanding, counsel, fortitude, knowledge, piety, fear of God) that you hold to govern me while I am yet here on Earth.

Scripture tells me, *"The Holy Spirit, whom the Father will send in my name, will teach you all things and will remind you of everything I have said to you"* (John 14:26, NIV).

I am humble and willing to learn; I thank You for having my back and keeping me on the straight and narrow. I know that the road of salvation is not easy, but I find assurance in knowing that You will always convict me concerning sin. I am so grateful that

You are my companion and are willing to be an active part of my life. I am thankful for the Holy Trinity, which completes me. Thank You, Holy Trinity, for being forever present in my life, working out all things for my good.

> *"Praise the LORD, my soul; all my inmost being, praise His holy name. Praise the LORD, my soul, and forget not all His benefits — who forgives all Your sins and heals all Your diseases, who redeems Your life from the pit and crowns You with love and compassion." Psalm 103:1-4 (NIV)*

Day 2

Thursday, September 2, 2021

Covering Me With Your Blessings

Entry One

Oh, Gracious Father, thank You for giving Evangelist Brown the insight to start this gratitude journal. I am elated that You have placed such a God-fearing woman into my life. Her obedience to Your will is admirable; this encourages me to be a better me in You.

You said in Your Word to, *"Walk in obedience to all that the Lord Your God has commanded you, so that you may live and prosper and prolong your days in the land that you will possess"* (Deut. 5:33, NIV).

Heavenly Father, I pledge to be obedient through the process of writing this journal of gratitude as the Holy Spirit leads me and guides me along the way. It is through this journal that I am permitted to allow my mind, body, and soul to focus on positive energy through a thankful lens. Your timing on all things is implacable. Thank You for knowing what I need, even when I am unaware of what my needs are.

Whatever You ask me to do, I trust You completely because I know that You will never ask anything of me that will harm me. Your Word confirms that when it says, *"'For I know the plans I have for you,' declares the Lord, 'plans to prosper you and not to harm you, plans to give you a hope and a future'"* (Jer. 29:11, NIV).

There is power in journaling my thoughts of gratitude. Where You lead me, I will follow because I know that all things are working for the good of me because I love the Lord. I am grateful that you show up in my life daily, ready to help me be my personal best for You.

Entry Two

Psalm 118:24 (ESV) says, "This is the day that the Lord has made; let us rejoice and be glad in it." Whether my day is filled with joy and peace or afflictions, I know that every day is the Lord's plan for my life. Thank you for reminding me that true peace comes from knowing that You are in control of all things. It is through the peace of God that will guard my heart against anxiety and focus my mind on what is good and pure. With much gratitude, I exalt my heavenly Father for His divine Word that strengthens me to walk in confidence, knowing that my inner atti-tude does not have to reflect my outward circumstances amid a chaotic society. I have no doubt that I can face anything through the strength of the almighty God.

Matthew 5:11-12 (NASB) reveals, *"Blessed are you when people insult you, persecute you and falsely say all kinds of evil against you because of me. Rejoice and be glad, because great is your reward in heaven, for in the same way they persecuted the prophets who were before you."*

When I became a child of God, I knew that I was not immune from the snares of the devil. The Word of God revealed to me that the world is in love with its own and because I am not of the world, the world hates me just like it hated Jesus. Thank you, God, for telling me the truth, letting me know that the world per-secuted Jesus and because I love Jesus, I will be persecuted also. Nevertheless, God promised to always be with me, remain faithful, give me power and purpose in my life, love me unconditionally, bring joy and hope to my life, and so much more. Consequently, I can walk in victory, knowing that my God is the Great I Am, the author and finisher of my faith and ruler of all things.

First Chronicles 16:5(NIV) says, *"For great is the Lord, and greatly to be praised; He also is to be feared above all gods."* I am grateful for this divine Word of comfort and hope which gives me something to look forward to. Thank You for being my strength amid my weakness. I praise, reverence, and adore you in Your infinite wisdom.

Entry Three

Heavenly Father, I am indebted and appreciative to You for the gift of prayer. Your Word tells me to, *"Pray without ceasing. In everything give thanks, for this is the will of God in Christ Jesus concerning You"* (1 Thess. 5:17-18, KJV).

I find comfort in knowing that You are always there willing, eager, and ready to listen to me. Prayer is my direct telephone line to You. When I call You, there is never an operator on the line, telling me You are too busy. God is always on the line and my prayers are answered just in time. Thank You for listening and hearing my prayers with a heart of love, grace, and tender loving compassion. I can air all of my dirty laundry before You, knowing that You will lift me above my circumstances and throw them in the sea of forgetfulness if I have a repentant heart.

When I go to You in prayer, Your Word declares, *"These things have I written unto You that believe on the name of the Son of God; that ye may know that ye have eternal life, and that ye may believe on the name of the Son of God. And this is the confidence that we have in Him, that, if we ask any thing according to his will, he heareth us: and if we know that he hear us, whatsoever we ask, we know that we have the petitions that we desired of him"* (1 John 5:13-15, KJV).

My prayer line to *You* means the world to me. I thank You for covering me with Your many blessings.

> *"Rejoice always, pray continually, give thanks in all circumstances; for this is God's will for You in Christ Jesus."* 1 Thessalonians 5:16-18 (NIV)

Day 3

Friday, September 3, 2021

El Shaddai – The All-Sufficient One

Entry One

Y ou are El Shaddai, God Almighty. Heavenly Father, I am so grateful that You are my All-Sufficient One, the supplier and provider of all my needs. *"I am the Alpha and the Omega," says the Lord God, "who is, and who was, and who is to come, the Almighty"* (Rev. 1:8, NIV).

Father God, You are the beginning and the end; everything revolves around You and Your perfect will. What an awesome God I serve. I express my deepest gratitude that You can triumph through every opposition or obstacle in my life, strengthening me to persevere till the end of time. I don't fear what the future holds because I know You hold the future. I can walk confidently into each day knowing that You are with me. Thank You for being my sustainer of all things. You are an astounding God.

Entry Two

El Shaddai, thank You for being my protector, dispatching Your angels, watching over me during the night, bringing me into a day that I have never seen before. I wake up each day with a zealous spirit, eager, and ready to face the unknown. It is a blessing to walk into this day with a new start, new possibilities because I know that You are by my side every step of the way. Your steadfast support means everything to me. It is through your unswerving love that extends from Earth to the heavens that keeps me entrenched in Your Word. I take refuge in the shadow of Your wings for You cover me and protect me like a mother hen covers her chicks.

"In peace I will lie down and sleep, for You alone, LORD, make me dwell in safety" (Ps. 4:8, NIV).

I appreciate You making sure that I am protected from all harm and danger. I am safe in You. Therefore, I can walk through good times or afflictions because I know that I'm covered in the blood of Jesus. Each day, I see Your grace which brings peace and hope for a brighter future, and I reverence You for supplying all of my needs according to Your riches in glory in Christ Jesus.

Entry Three

Oh, Gracious God, I thank You for the blood that runs warm through my veins, the very air that I breathe. "The Spirit of God has made me, And the breath of the Almighty gives me life" (Job 33:4, NIV). I know that someone did not wake up this morning because death knocked at their door, expiring them from this world to their next destination. My friend and co-worker in the educational system was battling the Corona virus. I took for granted that she would rise above this disease, come home, and continue her life. To my surprise, I got a telephone call, telling me that she passed. My heart grieved and I began to think how precious life is.

As I reflected on her passing, my heart grieved for there were so many things that I didn't get the opportunity to say. I realized that regrets for significant people in your life are one of the worst feelings in the world. The Spirit of God dealt with my mind and heart, convicting me and chastising me for not making the effort to bring peace amid a disjointed relationship. While there is nothing that I can do now, I have learned that life is too precious to take for granted. I embrace and am a believer to never put off today for tomorrow, for tomorrow is not promised to us. Thank You, God, for a lesson well learned.

"Finally, all of you, have unity of mind, sympathy, brotherly love, a tender heart, and a humble mind" (1 Pet. ESV).

Every second on the clock, someone is dying, but El Shaddai spared me. I choose to live this day to the fullest. God, thank You for giving me a hunger to not only listen and know Your Word, but a heart to practice Your Word in my daily living. I am so grateful that You have given me the breath of life this day. Help me to walk in my purpose and rejoice in it.

"Give thanks to the Lord, for he is good; his love endures forever" 1 Chronicles 16:34 (NIV)

Day 4

Saturday, September 4, 2021

Jehovah-Rapha – My Healer

Entry One

I am grateful that You are my Jehovah-Rapha, my healer. "You are the one who heals and forgives all of my sins and heals all of my diseases" (Ps. 103:3, NLT).

I thank You for Your divine Word that reminds me that You will always be there to restore my health and heal my wounds as declared by the Lord. I am appreciative of the love and care that You have for me. In Jeremiah 33:6 (NIV), You said, "I will bring health and healing to you; I will heal you and let You enjoy abundant peace and security."

I exalt You always for being present in my life, lifting me above the physical and emotional pain that can cause harm to my spiritual life. Thank You for filling me with the power of the Holy Spirit to bring healing to others. It is through You, heavenly Father that I can walk in the wholeness and newness of life today and forevermore until I have a perfected, holy, and fully healed body in Your presence in heaven.

Entry Two

To the great physician of all things; my granddaughter, Londyn who is five years old, woke up around 10:00 last night, September 3, 2021, screaming with excruciating pain in her stomach. She began to throw up ferociously running back and forth to the restroom, releasing waste from both ends of her body. I was filled with concern and compassion for my grandchild. I felt helpless and needed direction. My mind quickly went to panic mode and I began to think, "Could this be a manifestation of COVID-19." I thank the Holy Spirit for stepping in right at that very moment, reminding me that by Jesus' stripes, healing is in the atmosphere. I began to lay hands on Londyn, praying that God would remove this bitter cup from her body.

God's Word spoke to my heart, "Fear not, for I am with you; Be not dismayed for I am God. I will strengthen you, yes, I will help you, I will uphold you with my right hand of righteous" (Isa. 41:10, NKJV).

Within minutes, I could see a change in my granddaughter's countenance, strength in her eyes, and stamina in her body. I knew right at that very moment restoration had taken place through the redeeming blood of Jesus. I, then looked into Londyn's eyes, and said, "How are you feeling, are you alright?" She exclaimed, "I'm feeling fine!" I am exceedingly grateful to God for the deliverance, restoration, and healing of my grandchild. You are indeed Jehovah-Rapha.

Early the next morning, I heard Londyn muttering to herself. I asked her, "Are you talking to yourself?" She answered me with a voice of confidence and conviction, "I am praying to God because I forgot to say my prayers last night." Jehovah-Rapha, thank You for giving her a mind to know the importance of talking to You through prayer. We are grateful that through Your strength, we forged through the fire, knowing that You are preparing us for something greater.

Entry Three

Our God heals. Around thirty years of age, I was diagnosed with rheumatoid arthritis. I could remember it as if it were just yesterday. In the prime of my life and career, I got a call from the doctor's nurse while at work. She told me that the results had come back from my blood work confirming that I had rheumatoid arthritis. There was a long pause with extreme silence on the telephone. Suddenly, I heard my heart thumping with an intense rhythm as if it were going to explode. I mustarded up enough strength to say, "OK, thank you." Hanging up the telephone, I broke out in tears, sobbing with loud bursts of agony because I knew that rheumatoid arthritis was the worst kind of arthritis anyone could be diagnosed with; inflammation in the bloodstream flowing through my body. At that moment, I did not realize that, "With God all things are possible" (Matt. 19:26, NIV).

After wallowing in my pity, I finally came to myself through the unction of the Holy Spirit, realizing to whom I belong. I am a child of God and have access to all his blessings which are in heaven. My mind quickly transitioned from pity to faith, trust, assurance, deliverance, restoration, and healing. Each day, I began to walk in the wholeness of my life, knowing that God didn't bring me this far to leave me.

His Word reminds me that, "The Lord is my shield, giving grace and glory" (Ps. 84:11, NLT).

Each time I went to the doctor, he would check my vitals, request blood work, check my bone density, and had me perform strength tests with my hands. He was astounded that I was able to make the ball rise to the top despite my diagnosed condition, confessing that he would have a hard time doing what I did and didn't have arthritis. Look at God!

I found comfort in knowing that God promised me that, "He would restore my health, and heal my wounds; declares the Lord" (Jer. 30:7, NIV).

I am now sixty-two years of age, and each time I go to the doctor, he shakes his head with much perplexity in the wonder of how miraculous it is that I lead a fulfilling life with no hindrance

Dr. Rhonda A. Jaudon

to my quality of living. Where there is a miracle that cannot be explained, God is the explanation. My deliverance from rheumatoid arthritis is attributed to God and God alone. Thank You, Jehovah-Rapha, for lifting me above my afflictions into the realm of living an abundant life.

"O Lord my God, I cried out to You for help and You healed me." Psalm 30:2 (KJV)

Day 5

Sunday, September 5, 2021

El Elyon – The Most High God

Entry One

You are El Elyon, the Most High God; there is none like You. You are the King of kings, the Lord of lords. Every knee will bow, and every tongue will confess that You are Lord. Dear, God, I find comfort in knowing that I serve a God that has the highest sovereignty over heaven and earth. You created this world; therefore, You have full authority to do whatever You desire.

Psalms 57:2 (ESV) says, "I cry out to God Most High, to God who fulfills his purpose for me."

I worship, exalt, praise, and give thanks to You, El Elyon, who loves me so much that You took the time to create the heavens and the earth for my dwelling. When I think of Your name, I am amazed at how it transcends time. You are over all situations, possessor over the heavens and the earth, name above all names, Lord of hosts, and a God that performs all things. With much gratitude, I appreciate You making a sacrifice of love (death, burial, and resurrection of Jesus) to permit me to be a part of Your divine royal family. With all my heart, I thank You for being my rock and my redeemer in all situations.

Entry Two

Not only did You create this world for my enjoyment, but You have also blessed my life through the years. I remember sitting in the project window at eleven or twelve years of age, looking down at the chaos that surrounded me. I began to cry out to God to find a way for me to go to college because my mother could not afford it as she was a single mother raising eight kids. I wanted a life different from what I saw and knew. In my mind, college was the answer to making that happen. I made a promise to God that if He would make a way for me to go to college, I would seek after Him and serve Him. I began church hopping from one church to another, seeking to get to know God and studying His Word. God saw my heart and had tender loving compassion for my condition. I am appreciative to God for making it possible for me to receive scholarships and grants to pay for my college tuition. I now hold four degrees. In 2016, I received my doctorate degree in Instructional and Organizational Leadership from Grand Canyon University. I give God all the praises, honor, and glory for this would not have been possible had it not been for Him blessing my path.

"Take delight in the Lord, and he will give you the desires of your heart" (Ps. 37:4, NIV).

If God did this for me, I know that He will do the same for you and perhaps far greater blessings. I encourage the body of Christ to seek God, the One who performs all and can give you your heart's desires. What an awesome God we serve.

Entry Three

When God created this world, he strategically picked my mother, placed me in her wound, and carefully molded and made me into a living being. While my mother was a single parent raising eight children, she walked with dignity, self-worth, and an unspeakable amount of strength. She loved the Lord and encouraged her children to develop a relationship with God. Many nights, I would watch her sitting on the edge of her bed with sadness and tears in her eyes, wondering how bills would be paid. She would always remind me that God will make a way out of no way. I didn't know what she meant at that time, but as I grew older, I came to the knowledge of the fullest of its meaning. In other words, my mother was telling me that God can do the impossible, and could change the unchangeable.

"Behold, I am the Lord, the God of all flesh; is anything too difficult for Me" (Jer. 32:27, NASB).

My mother has gone on to glory but her spirit is forever present with me. I am extremely grateful to God for giving me a strong, disciplinary, and loving mother to keep me on track. Assigning her as my mother was not designed by accident; she was purposefully assigned to me by God. I thank you, Lord, for all of my experiences, and I would not exchange anything because each experience shaped me into the person I have become.

> *"In Him we also have obtained an inheritance, having been predestined according to the purpose of Him who works all things in accordance with the plan of His will." Ephesians 1:11 (NIV)*

Day 6

Monday, September 6, 2021

Jehovah Nissi – God, My Banner

Entry One

Merciful Father, You are Jehovah Nissi, God, my banner. I am so grateful that I serve a God that triumphs over all things. It is a blessing to serve a God that gives me hope and focus through His divine Word while in this world. I give thanks to You, oh God, for giving me victory through Jesus Christ.

Exodus 17:15 (KJV) states, "And Moses built an altar and named it, 'The LORD Is My Banner.'"

I am aware that I am in a battle with the kingdom of darkness each day of my life. Nonetheless, I can walk in each day knowing that You are my banner, my battle standard. Thank You, Jehovah Nissi for reminding me that "the battle is not mine, it is Yours saith the Lord" (2 Chron 20:15, NIV). I am a foreigner, passing through Earth with a purpose-driven assignment from on high. When my enemies come against me, I will fight the battle on my knees, knowing that I am victorious through You. I show gratitude for God's presence and power that is always working for my good, winning the battles of sin and darkness over my life.

Praise Be To God who says, "No weapon that is formed against thee shall prosper; and every tongue that shall rise against thee in judgment thou shalt condemn. This is the heritage of the servants of the LORD, and their righteousness is of me, saith the LORD" (Isa. 54:17, KJV).

Jehovah Nissi, You are to be exalted in all things.

Entry Two

Jehovah Nissi, I give thanks to You for covering me in the blood of Jesus throughout my life. As a child, I was in bondage in my mind, holding on to family secrets that imprisoned me from life and liberty. I was fighting inner darkness in my life that was sheer hell for me. I felt guilty and that I deserved what happened to me. I was ashamed, felt dirty, and unworthy to be loved. In my dark hours of dealing with molestation as a young girl, You stepped in and assured me that it wasn't my fault, releasing me from the bondage, giving me victory, restoring my emotional mindset, and placing my feet on solid ground. I overflow with increasing gratitude for Your constant presence in my life.

Galatians 5:1 (NIV) affirms, "For freedom Christ has set us free; stand firm therefore, and do not submit again to a yoke of slavery." Heavenly Father, You are my saving grace. I give thanks to You for breaking this stronghold in my life.

Entry Three

In Jehovah Nissi, I am complete because I was given an identity when You made me Your child. I thank You for Your unwavering faith in me and for transforming me to look more like You. I exalt You to the highest as You are the one, true, living God, and I desire to walk in Your image. When I am unsure of myself, You make me strong and steady, strengthening me amid my weakness. Thank you for covering me with Your banner of love and for Your constant presence in my life.

Romans 8:35-39 (NASB) asks, "Who shall separate us from the love of Christ? Shall trouble or hardship or persecution or famine or nakedness or danger or sword? As it is written: For Your sake we face death all day long; we are considered as sheep to be slaughtered."

Transforming My Attitude Through Gratitude

In all these things, we are more than conquerors through him who loved us. "For I am convinced that neither death nor life, neither angels nor demons, neither the present nor the future, nor any powers, neither height nor depth, nor anything else in all creation, will be able to separate us from the love of God that is in Christ Jesus our Lord" (Rom. 8:38-39, NIV). This scripture is a blessed assurance for I pledge to let nothing separate me from You. Help me remain humble and confident in following the plans You have for my life. I am grateful for Your patience in allowing me to take one step at a time. I count it a blessing that You are always there when I need You. Thank You for Your protection and grace.

"So shall they fear the name of the Lord from the west, and his glory from the rising of the sun. When the enemy shall come in like a flood, the Spirit of the Lord shall lift up a standard against him." Isaiah 59:19 (KJV)

Day 7

Tuesday, September 7, 2021

Adonai – Lord and Master Over All Things

Entry One

Almighty God, I come before You with praise. You are Adonai, master, owner, and Lord of over all things. All other names must bow down to Your name for You are our foundation in Jesus Christ. I count it a blessing that You are Lord and master over my life. Because of Your Lordship over my life, when the wind, storm, rain, darkness, afflictions, and trouble are at my door, I can stand because I can do all things through You who strengthens me. Thank You, God, for Your divine Word that keeps me rooted in You. I am grateful that You sent the Holy Spirit to give me a mind to study Your Word, meditating on it day and night as it transforms the renewing of my mind. You are the creator of this world. Therefore, You have the right to rule and reign over all things that dwell within. I acknowledge Your divine authority and give thanks for all that You are in my life. I count it all joy and am filled with gratitude for Your presence in my life. You are holy, merciful, loving, gracious, kind, just, righteous, faithful, and so much more. Who wouldn't want to serve a God that has shown unconditional love for His children, even amid a sinful nature.

Your Word says, "Love is patient and kind; love does not envy or boast; it is not arrogant or rude. It does not insist on its own way; it is not irritable or resentful; it does not rejoice at wrongdoing, but rejoices with the truth. Love bears all things, believes all things, hopes all things, endures all things" (1 Cor. 13:4-7, ESV).

Thank You, Adonai, for teaching me how to love.

Entry Two

I am indebted to Adonai for His mercy and His grace in my life. In my sinful nature, I deserve eternal judgment, but when I show a grateful heart, He is faithful to forgive and continues to overflow my cup with blessings. Thank You, Adonai, for blessing me with the gift of teaching students and motivating educators to attain their personal best in the classroom. I have been given a blessed talent from on High. I get paid for something I love to do that I would do for free. I have worked as a teacher and administrator for forty-plus years with the Glynn County School System. Every triumph and milestone I have made is not of my own efforts but that of Adonai's blessings. Without Him, I can do nothing, but with Him, I can do all things. Thank You for making the desires of my heart possible. I give You all the praise honor and glory for Your role in my professional career and all the people that You put in my pathway to help me be successful!

The Word of God says, "Commit your works to the Lord and your plans will be established" (Prov. 16:3, KJV).

Entry Three

There have been times in my life when I felt a present void, weak, hopeless, spending time doing things to fill the void. But to no avail, that constant emptiness continued to reside in me. With that being said, I was setting myself up for attacks by Satan, leading me into danger that could result in sin which leads to death and destruction. It is a blessing that Adonai reached down in my darkest moment and pulled me out filling that God-sized hole that so much needed His loyalty with unconditional love and comfort.

John 14:10 (ESV) says, "Don't you believe that I am in the Father, and that the Father is in me? The Words I say to you I do not speak on my own authority. Rather, it is the Father, living in me, who is doing his work."

I give thanks to Adonai, the one who rules and reigns over my life. I am grateful for both His love and chastisement as He shapes and molds me to His specification, preparing the way for me to walk in His will for my life.

> *"Adonai bless you and keep you! Adonai make His face to shine on you and be gracious to you! Adonai turn His face toward you and grant you shalom" (Num. 6:24-26 (NIV).*

Day 8

Wednesday, September 8, 2022

Jehovah Jireh – The Lord Who Provides

Entry One

Good morning, Jehovah Jireh. I woke up this morning with thanksgiving in my heart. I am extremely grateful to the All-Sufficient God who surrounds me with His love, friendship, and protection. I'm convinced that no one on this earth can love me the way God loves and adores me, despite my shortcomings. Heavenly Father, thank You for being my spiritual daddy, giving me the resources and care I need to live an abundant life. I walk into today and tomorrow because I know that You are my Lord who holds my future and provides for my many needs. I appreciate You putting angels in charge of protecting me from all harm and danger, a constant help in time of need.

You are a God that not only sees all, but You see things before they take place and make provisions for my needs. While I am aware that I am an imperfect creature, You keep loving, protecting, and making provisions for me daily. Even to the point that You were willing to sacrifice Your Son for me, "The lamb slain from the foundation of the world" (Rev. 13:8, NIV).

Thank You, Jehovah, for taking care of me and reminding me of Your goodness. Matthew 6:26 (NIV) says, "Look at the birds of the air, that they do not sow, nor reap nor gather into barns, and yet your heavenly Father feeds them. Are you not worth much more than they?"

I am grateful that You find me worthy of You for I am set apart as special in Your eyes. Your love for me does not go unnoticed. You are superlative, my Jehovah Jireh.

Entry Two

I grew up in very humble beginnings. While living in the country, I didn't have the niceties that were afforded to some people. There were eight siblings in the house with only two bedrooms. In the children's room, there were two beds, four children in each bed. Needless to say, it was quite uncomfortable as I reminisce on this time in my life. We didn't have an inside bathroom, so we had to go to the outhouse located adjacent to our house. I was often scared because snakes roamed about with no respect for person or property. Can you imagine? Snakes are my greatest fear. We didn't have running water in the home, and one of my jobs was to get the wagon and walk at least a mile or so to my Uncle Will's house to get water from the well. We didn't have a bathtub in the home, so we bathed in a tub in the middle of the living room near the stove to keep warm. Despite my conditions, God protected my mind. In my mind, this was normal for I was truly unaware that I was poor.

Romans 12:22 (ESV) tells us, "Do not be conformed to this world, but be transformed by the renewal of your mind, that by testing you may discern what is the will of God, what is good and acceptable and perfect."

God provided for my needs and sustained my life, bridging it to a greater future. Looking over this situation, I see the blessings at hand, even amid hardships, God was building my character in preparation to walk in my future. All of this was working for my good. I now live in a beautiful home on Oak Grove Island with all the niceties that Jehovah Jireh has provided for me.

Truly, "My God will supply all your needs according to His riches in glory in Christ Jesus" (Phil. 4:19, NIV).

Entry Three

As a child, I didn't have fond memories of my father as I watched him disrespect my mother, beating her and mentally abusing her. In my mind, he was a demon. But what I do know is I didn't want to ever be married to someone who didn't show love for me and respected me as his wife. My Jehovah knew that I carried this demon memory in my mind from childhood to my adulthood.

Jehovah says in his Word, "Be strong and courageous. Do not be afraid or terrified because of them, for the LORD your God goes with you; he will never leave you nor forsake you" (Deut. 31:6, NIV).

Even then, God was looking out for me, making provisions for my future. On the perfect day at the perfect time, I met my future husband, right before I was set to graduate from Georgia Southern College. I thank God for sending Robert into my life who shows love for me and doing thoughtful things for me to show that he cares.

"For the Lord God is a sun and shield: the Lord will give grace and glory: no good thing will he withhold from them that walk uprightly." Jeremiah 84:11 (KJV

33

Day 9

Thursday, September 9, 2021

Jehovah Shalom: The God of Peace

Entry One

How awesome it is to be among the living. Thank You for allowing me to be a part of such a glorious day. I come before You, Jehovah-Shalom; the God of peace, seeking Your face for wisdom, knowledge, and guidance as I deal with life experiences. It is through You that I can confront afflictions with a peaceful spirit that surpasses all understanding in this world. In the fullness of Your peace, I am empowered to pull down strongholds in my life and the lives of Your people who are in need. I give You praise, honor, and glory for putting praise in my spirit, knowing that You will fight my battles and keep me elevated above ungodly circumstances of the world.

The Word of God tells me, "Do not be anxious about anything, but in every situation, by prayer and petition, with thanksgiving, present your requests to God. And the peace of God, which transcends all understanding, will guard your hearts and your minds in Christ Jesus" (Phil. 4:6-7, NIV).

I am so grateful to Jehovah Shalom for blessing me, smiling on me, being gracious to me, and giving me His peace. I walk in Your favor this day.

Entry Two

In John 14:27 (NIV), Jehovah Shalom reminds me, "Peace I leave with you; my peace I give you. I do not give to you as the world gives. Do not let your hearts be troubled and do not be afraid."

One of my greatest fears was losing my mother. I dreaded the thought of being in this world without her. Nevertheless, when it was time for my mother to transition from the world to glory, God stepped in and reminded me of His peace and love that will sustain me through all things. Much to my surprise, I didn't feel the agony of pain, stress, or depression, but instead felt joy, praise, and peace because I knew that my mother was in a better place.

The scripture says, "We are confident, yes, well pleased rather to be absent from the body and to be present with the Lord." (2 Cor. 5:8, NKJV).

Knowing that my mother is with the Lord gives me insurmountable peace and joy. Thank You, Jehovah Shalom, for giving her to me for a moment in time. Her presence in my life will always be dear to my heart, but I could never love her the way You do. I am so grateful for Your perfect peace.

Entry Three

At this present moment, we are experiencing a worldwide pandemic that is running rampant in society. This dreadful disease from the pits of hell is claiming millions and millions of lives, leaving families destitute, dismantled, discounted, full of fear, and full of pain. The world as we know it is gone and we are now experiencing a new normal. I chose not to embrace the worldview but look at this pandemic through the kingdom or spiritual view. I walk through this period with caution and wisdom; I refuse to be consumed with fear.

2 Timothy 1:7 (KJV) reveals, "God hath not given us the spirit of fear; but of power, and of love, and of a sound mind."

I serve a God that is bigger than all circumstances and can change the unchangeable. I know that I am blessed and covered by the blood of Jesus. Jehovah Shalom will help us come out of the pandemic better not bitter, peace not fear, and whole, not broken. No matter how dark it gets, I am grateful to God for giving me hope and peace as I look forward to a brighter tomorrow.

> *"Let the peace of Christ rule in your hearts, since as members of one body You were called to peace. And be thankful. Let the message of Christ dwell among you richly as you teach and admonish one another with all wisdom through psalms, hymns, and songs from the Spirit, singing to God with gratitude in your hearts. And whatever you do, whether in word or deed, do it all in the name of the Lord Jesus, giving thanks to God the Father through him." Colossians 3:15-17 (NIV)*

Day 10

Friday, September 10, 2021

Jehovah Rohi: The Lord Is My Shepherd

Entry One

"The Lord is my shepherd; I shall not want. He maketh me to lie down in green pastures. He leadeth me beside the still waters. He restoreth my soul: he leadeth me in the paths of righteousness for his name's sake" (Ps. 23:1-3, KJV).

Jehovah Rohi, I give total praise and thanks to You for being the peaceful shepherd in my life. When I am going through the storms, trials, and the test of times, I am grateful that You are the One that guides me through. You are a lamp unto my feet and a light unto my path.

Isaiah 40:11 (NASB 1995) tells, "Like a shepherd He will tend His flock, in His arm He will gather the lambs and carry them in His bosom."

Jehovah Rohi, I love You and I trust You completely with knowing the necessities that I need to live a Godly life. During the entire span of my life, I have witnessed You heal the sick, restore failure, elevate the humble, forgive sinners, bless the poor, defend the weak, right the wrongs and so much more. My highest gratitude is bestowed unto You for finding it not robbery to take care of the welfare of Your children. I praise an awesome God.

Entry Two

I give allegiance to You, my Shepherd, that provides all the nourishment that we need to sustain us during our earthly dwelling as we wait for the glorious day that we will live and reign with You forever. Thank You, Jehovah Rohi, for placing it in my heart to take the time to visit Altama Elementary School's faculty and staff members. They recently lost a teacher to COVID and before her death, two other faculty members passed away and a host of students' parents.

As I walked into the building, I felt a heaviness of gloom and sadness. I am grateful to Jehovah for using me as an instrument to minister to Your people, lifting their spirits in a time of need. You are indeed the true Shepherd of all things. As I walked from one classroom to the other, we prayed, we talked, we laughed, we hugged, and we simply loved each other. After visiting the final classroom, I walked down the hall, witnessing a different feeling in the atmosphere. I no longer felt the gloom, doom, and sadness for it had instantly transitioned to a peace that surpasses all understanding.

At that very moment, I knew that my Shepherd and my Lord had provided the healing medicine needed to shift the atmosphere. Psalm 34:18 (NIV) says, "The Lord is close to the brokenhearted and saves those who are crushed in spirit."

While this school has gone through the test of time, they have forged through the fire as a result of the Great Shepherd of heaven and earth. He stepped in and mended the broken hearts. Thank You, Jehovah Rohi for being the constant help in time of need. You are a right on time, God.

Entry Three

Around 1966, my parents separated and later divorced. During this time, I yearned for my father to take an interest in me and my well-being. Every child looks forward to being nourished by their parents to fulfill the various needs in their lives. To much dismay, he never came around to check on me, didn't provide financial support, or assist my mother in putting food on the table. In short, he ghosted himself from my life completely. The need for him to be present in my life suddenly turned into a broken heart filled with resentment, anger, and disdain. Anytime, someone called His name or referred to me as his daughter, I cringed and wanted to scream from the top of my voice, "HE IS NOT MY DADDY!"

At a young and tender age in my life, I came to know Jehovah Rohi, my Shepherd who made me and knows all about me, even the number of hairs on my head. How awesome is that to have a Savior that is so connected with you that he knows your every thought and is willing and ready to provide for all of your needs. God's Word spoke to me, "Be kind to one another, tenderhearted, forgiving one another, as God in Christ forgave you" (Eph. 4:32, ESV).

Amid my broken heart, my anger, my disdain, my pain, He touched my heart and reminded me that He loves me and is constantly working on my behalf. He instructed me to turn my thoughts from resentment, anger, and pain and turn them toward Him who can sustain me, deliver me, restore me, and keep me from falling.

The Word of God says, "Do not let the sun go down while you are still angry and don give the devil a foothold" (Eph. 4:26-27, NIV).

"Get rid of all bitterness, rage and anger, brawling and slander, along with every form of malice" (Eph. 4:31, NIV).

As a result, I began to experience a transformed heart and mind using love as a barometer for change in my attitude and disposition. Instead of resentment and bitterness toward my daddy, I allowed the seeds of love and reconciliation to grow in my heart that pointed to my Shepherd because I couldn't do it on my own. Lord, I thank You for protecting me, guiding me, mending my wounds, and blessing me throughout my life. As I journey through this phase of my life, help me to faithfully follow You, and remind me to focus my time and energy on recognizing all the blessings in my life as a result of Your unconditional love. Because I am rooted in You, no matter what my circumstances, I know that You care for me. In that, I find absolute comfort and security in knowing that my Lord and Shepherd is in control and working things out for my good. I am grateful.

"Behold, the Lord GOD will come with strong hand, and his arm shall rule for him: behold, his reward is with him, and his work before him. He shall feed his flock like a shepherd: he shall gather the lambs with his arm, and carry them in his bosom, and shall gently lead those that are with young."
Isaiah 40:10-11 (KJV)

Day 11

Saturday, September 11, 2021

Jehovah Uzi: God Is Our Refuge And Strength

Entry One

I come before You, Jehovah-Uzi, for You are my strength now and forever. Your Word declares, "God is our refuge and strength, a very present help in trouble. Therefore, will not we fear, though the earth be removed, and though the mountains be carried into the midst of the sea. Though the waters thereof roar and be troubled, though the mountains shake with the swelling thereof. Selah," (Ps. 46:1-3, KJV).

I am grateful that You have given me this assurance that I can find strength in You. I trust You, Jehovah, with all my heart and I rejoice and praise You for Your constant presence in my life. I can face all adversities, afflictions, and difficult times in my life because You are mightier than all my circumstances, my rock.

I'm reminded of David in the book of Psalms; no matter what David was going through in his life or what was going on around him, he had faith without any doubt that he was under God's protection and provision. Comparatively speaking, I have no doubt that I am a child of God, and I too am strengthened by His promise during the weak moments in my life. With an outpouring of gratitude unto Jehovah-Uzi, thank You for being strong when I'm weak.

Entry Two

I am reminded of a student that stole money from another student at school. When confronted about the situation, he made up an elaborate story on how he got the money. Each lie turned into a bigger lie; by the end of the story, he didn't know where the truth began, and the lie ended. I shared with the student that if I couldn't find the underlying cause of the truth, I would have to involve the school resource officer. This, in turn, frightened the student, and when he went home, he told his parents an elaborate lie on me.

This resulted in the parents threatening to take a lawsuit out on me due to defamation of character. During this long wait, there were so many things going through my mind. Even though I was innocent, I allowed worry and fear to creep in, sucking the strength out of me. It concerned me greatly as I was retiring within months, and I didn't want to end my retirement with such a negative tone over my head. Praise to the Most High God that this incident didn't go any further than a mere threat.

I found comfort in God's Word which states, "These things I have spoken unto You, that in me ye might have peace. In the world ye shall have tribulation: but be of good cheer; I have overcome the world" (John 16:33, KJV).

In my weakest moment, Jehovah Uzi stepped in and assured me that He is my strength in the time of weakness. The tension that occupied my body was slowly released and I could feel a peace that came over me. Thank You, Jehovah, for lifting me above my circumstances and reminding me to trust You no matter what is seen with my carnal eye.

Entry Three

Trusting God involves surrendering unto Him and believing in the reliability, truth, and strength of what can be achieved through the power and might of God. The Bible affirms that we serve a God that cannot lie; He always keeps His promises, "Fear thou not; for I am with thee: be not dismayed; for I am thy God: I will strengthen thee; yea, I will help thee; yea, I will uphold thee with the right hand of my righteousness" (Isa. 41:10, KJV).

We can lean and depend on God to sustain us in all things. Jehovah-Uzi, I thank You for being there for me amid doubting times, sending the Holy Spirit to remind me of the reliability of Your Word and the strength in You that comes with it. I am reminded of Job, a faithful and devout Christian who put his faith and trust in the will and strength of God. Job lost everything: his children, his wealth, his livestock, his crops, his health, and even the relationship of his wife and friends.

After such tragedy, "Job got up and tore his robe and shaved his head. Then he fell to the ground in worship and said: "Naked I came from my mother's womb, and naked I will depart.

The LORD gave and the LORD has taken away; may the name of the LORD be praised" (Job 1:20-21, NIV).

Job's commitment and reliance on the strength of God were such a blessing to my spirit. It helped to increase my gratitude to Jehovah for standing by my side and reminding me that I don't have to face hard times on my own for He is there with me. You are an incredible God; there is none like You.

"My flesh and my heart may fail, but God is the strength of my heart and my portion forever." Psalm 73:26 (ESV)

Day 12

Sunday, September 12, 2021

Jehovah-M'kaddesh: The God of Sanctification

Entry One

I come before You today, lifting Your name that is great and powerful over all names. Without You, God, sanctification does not exist for You are the only God that has the power to sanctify, Jehovah-M'kaddesh. God's divine Word tells us that sanctification is the will of God; the process of being cleansed from our sins and becoming more like Christ Jesus.

Leviticus 20:7-8 unveils to us, "Sanctify yourselves therefore, and be ye holy: for I am the Lord your God. And ye shall keep my statutes, and do them: I am the Lord which sanctify you."

I am so grateful to You for making it possible to purify my heart and mind through confession, repentance, acceptance, prayer, and spiritual experiences. I can come boldly before the throne of Grace because of Your sanctifying grace that You have bestowed upon me, even though, I am unworthy of it. Your grace and mercy is a remarkable act of unconditional love.

"In Him we have redemption through his blood, the forgiveness of sins, in accordance with the riches of God's grace" (Eph. 1:7, NIV).

Entry Two

During this worldwide pandemic of COVID-19, many lives have been claimed as a result of this plague that has fallen upon us. I can't help but think about how many lives have been snatched from this world by Satan that did not give their lives to God. With that being said, there is an urgency for saints to spread the gospel of salvation to all that will hear it.

"Then saith he unto his disciples, The harvest truly is plenteous, but the labourers are few; Pray ye therefore the Lord of the harvest, that he will send forth labourers into his harvest" (Matt. 9:37-38, KJV).

Salvation and sanctification through Jehovah M'Kaddesh is the only way to sustain us for all eternity. We can't go back and correct the past, but we can, at this point, allow God to use us as His vessels to make sure that the people of God accept Christ Jesus before their time is up here on Earth.

Oh, gracious God, "In Him we have redemption through his blood, the forgiveness of sins, in accordance with the riches of God's grace" (Eph. 1:7, NIV).

With an overflowing of gratitude, I give thanks to You for the redemption of my sins through the substitutionary lamb of Your Son, Jesus Christ – sanctification is possible.

Entry Three

As I look back over my life, I can truly say that I've been blessed and protected even when I didn't truly know God in His fullness. I come from the core of poverty, chaos, surrounded by sinful experiences that could have easily shaped my future toward destruction, attempting to steal my chance for salvation.

God's Word says, "'No weapon forged against you will prevail, and you will refute every tongue that accuses you. This is the heritage of the servants of the Lord, and this is their vindication from me,' declares the Lord." (Isa. 54:17, NIV).

I am grateful that Jehovah-M'kaddesh had His hand on me, molding, and making me into something greater that He destined in my life. I'm extremely grateful to the only wise God that forgave me of my iniquities, cleansed me of my sins, and sanctified me so that I could walk in His glory.

> *"I appeal to you therefore, brothers, by the mercies of God, to present your bodies as a living sacrifice, holy and acceptable to God, which is your spiritual worship. Do not be conformed to this world, but be transformed by the renewal of your mind, that by testing you may discern what is the will of God, what is good and acceptable and perfect." Romans 12:1-2 (ESV)*

Day 13

Monday, September 13, 2021

Immanuel: God With Us

Entry One

Matthew 1:22-23 (NIV) declares, "The virgin will be with child and will give birth to a son, and they will call him Immanuel—which means, God with us." Oh, how great and powerful is Immanuel; I am exceptionally grateful that You are with me always even unto the end of the world.

Scripture says, "Behold, I am with you and will keep you wherever you go, and will bring you back to this land. For I will not leave you until I have done what I have promised you" (Gen. 28:15, NIV).

Without Jesus' birth, death, burial, and resurrection, there would be no salvation, making my pathway hell-bound. I burst with gratitude that You love me so much that You allowed Your Son to lay down His life for me, an undeserving sinner. There is nothing that I can ever experience in my life that You don't understand because I serve a God that is all-knowing and all-seeing.

Entry Two

I'm reminded of the song, "Immanuel," written by Michael Card, "A sign shall be given; a virgin will conceive; a human baby bearing undiminished deity. The glory of the nations; a light for all to see that hope for all who will embrace His warm reality, Immanuel."

Dear God, You are the light of the world, a present help in time of need. You are my light amid darkness, peace in the middle of chaos, joy amid sorrow as well as a friend when I'm friendless. I am grateful to You for giving me hope now and in the future.

Your Word declares, "May the God of hope fill you with all joy and peace as you trust in Him, so that you may overflow with hope by the power of the Holy Spirit" (Rom. 15:13, NIV).

When You call me, I will answer as I know Your voice like a baby knows the voice of its dad. I desire to be obedient to the plans that You have for my life. I am no longer afraid of the evil that resides in this world because if You are for me, then who dares to come against me. My loyalty is in You, Immanuel, my Lord and Savior.

Entry Three

Around midnight on Saturday, September 11, 2021, the Holy Spirit gave me some insight into the letters of the name Immanuel: As I looked at the letters in the name, I recognized the blessings that come from Him in the acrostic below:

Incredible; involved in every detail in my life, plans my future.
Master of unconditional love despite my sins.
Merciful and full of grace. A God of second chances.
Amazing, advocate that makes provisions for me.
Nurturer when I'm at my lowest point; wipes my tears.
Understanding and caring about my needs.
Everlasting; prepares a place for me for all eternity.
Love overflows with limitless blessings.

My gratitude toward Immanuel who is present and alive in my life is hard for me to explain. Each time I think about what You are to me, I realize that there is no number of words to describe

Your infinite being. You are the magnificent, majestic, miraculous, Most High God. Thank You for loving me.

"I will give thanks to the Lord with all my heart; I will tell of all Your wonders." Psalm 9:1 (NASB 1995)

Day 14

Tuesday, September 14, 2021

Jehovah Tsidkenu: The God of Righteousness

Entry One

Jesus is our Jehovah Tsidkenu; the God of righteousness. Your righteousness is more than a characteristic; it is Your fulfillment of the covenant and promises that You have made for Your glory. Your Word tells us, "I am the Lord, who exercises kindness, justice and righteousness on earth, for in these I delight" (Jer. 9:24, NIV).

I'm grateful, God, that I not only know that You are righteous, but I have experienced what Your righteousness looks like in the fullness of Your glory. There have been people in my life that have been unkind, unfair, and unjust. While it seemed that they were on the top of their game at that time, the day came when You turned things around for me. I am grateful to You for showing me how to look through the spiritual lens and see Your hand in it, rejoicing and praising You every step of the way.

While I cannot earn righteousness, I am grateful that You became my righteousness which is earned through You. When I complain, help me to be mindful that I am not alone as I struggle with life situations. Your Word tells me, "God is with you – wherever You may go and no matter what life brings" (Josh. 1:9, NIV).

Thank You for making it possible for me to live a righteous life through You, my Jehovah-Tsidkenu. Proverbs tells us about using Godly wisdom to help us choose between what is right and what is wrong. I am extremely thankful that You have given me the Holy Spirit to convict, lead, and guide me through life experiences. What a Mighty God we serve.

Entry Two

Father God, I give You all the praise, honor, and glory for being my God of righteousness. Mankind tends to have somewhat of a self-righteous tone, especially when he or she thinks that they are correct and validated by something. They refuse to listen, shut down, argue their point, become indignant, and feel that they have a right to defend themselves. But what we fail to realize is that it's not about what we think is right but what God deems is right.

Father God, I repent of my part in rendering a self-righteous tone; I desire to live a righteous and humble life through You. Thank You for Your promise to me when You say, "Blessed are those who hunger and thirst for righteousness, for they shall be satisfied" (Matt. 5:6, ESV).

In You, Jehovah Tsidkenu, I am complete; thank You for giving me the spirit of discernment to choose right over wrong, using Your Godly flow map for living a life that is righteous and pleasing in Your sight.

Entry Three

"For Christ also suffered once for sins, the righteous for the unrighteous, that he might bring us to God, being put to death in the flesh but made alive in the spirit" (1 Pet. 3:18, ESV).

Oh Merciful God, I confess that I am a sinner saved by Your grace. With much gratitude, I exalt the God of righteousness for taking on my sins; the one who is righteous, holy, and perfect in all things; a God who became sin for me to give me a right to salvation. What an amazing sacrifice.

I want to live a life that is faithful unto You and be made righteous in Your sight. I'm reminded of Abraham who was willing to give up his son ,Isaac, on the altar as a perfect sacrifice to God. His faith in God was unwavering no matter what the cost, which made him righteous in the sight of God. Abraham was recognized as the "Father of faith." Heavenly Father, I want to live a life before You with abundant faith in all things. When my faith is weak, I pray that you strengthen me.

> *"For Your righteousness, O God, reaches to the heavens, You who have done great things; O God, who is like You?"*
> *Psalm 71:19 (NIV)*

Day 15

Wednesday, September 15, 2021

Jehovah-Bara: The Lord, The Creator

Entry One

J ehovah-Bara, I am blessed to have You in my life, the Lord, the Creator. You are so high, I can't go over You, so low I can't go under You, and so wide, I can't go around You. I must come in at the door. Your Word says, "Here I am! I stand at the door and knock. If anyone hears my voice and opens the door, I will come in and eat with that person, and they with me" (Rev. 3:20, NIV).

You are the everlasting God, Alpha and Omega, the beginning and the end, the creator of all the earth and everything that dwells therein. Mankind can create things that already exist, but God is the only one that can create something out of nothing. He spoke the entire universe into existence.

In the book of Genesis, scripture reveals, "In the beginning God created the heavens and the earth The earth was a formless void and darkness covered the face of the deep, while a wind from God swept over the face of the waters. Then God said, "let there be light" and there was light" (Gen. 1:1-3, ESV).

Father God, I am grateful that You created everything in this world for my enjoyment. All that You ask is that I serve with all my heart, soul, and mind. Even before the beginning of time, You had me in mind. Thank You for always taking care of me.

Entry Two

After You carefully created the world and everything within it, You decided to make me. I am grateful that You prepared the way for me with all the niceties to take care of my needs before bringing me into this world.

In Genesis 1:26 (ESV), God said, "Let us make mankind in our image, in our likeness, so that they may rule over the fish in the sea and the birds in the sky, over the livestock and all the wild animals, and over all the creatures that move along the ground."

Jehovah-Bara, I am grateful that You created me out of love with the intent for me to show love for my brothers and sisters in Christ Jesus. I was made in the likeness of Your image to live a life that is reflective of You and the way You take care of this world and all Your people. You have been faithful to me in all things and I thank You, sincerely.

Entry Three

Heavenly Father, when You created me; You had a perfect plan for my life declaring that I am a refugee passing through this world on an assignment from You and You alone. Thank You for giving me purpose, nothing happens in my life by chance. Whether the experiences were good or bad, I walk away richer and wiser as I learn from my failures. It is through my failures that I learn what it means to trust in Jesus. As a result, I can build character and persevere to the end. You are the great orchestrator over all things, working things out for my good.

Psalms 57:2 (ESV) says, "I cry out to God Most High, to God who fulfills his purpose for me."

I know that You have numbered my days here on Earth. My prayer is that I walk in the plan You have for my life faithfully, fulfilling every purpose You have for me. As I live this purpose-driven life, You have given me the gift of educating children and helping others to become their personal best. Thank You for Your eternal guidance and loving hand in my life. I can't imagine life without You; the creator, author, and finisher of my faith.

"You alone are the Lord. You made the heavens, even the highest heavens, and all their starry host, the earth and all that is on it, the seas and all that is in them. You give life to everything, and the multitudes of heaven worship You." Nehemiah 9:6 (NIV)

Day 16

Thursday, September 16, 2021

Jehovah-Sabaoth: The Lord of Hosts

Entry One

I come before Jehovah Sabaoth, the Lord of Hosts, giving You praise and exaltations for who You are in my life. You are the Lord of Powers that has Lordship over all things in the heavens and the earth and anything else in between. When the armies of difficulties come into my life, I can be still because I serve a God who will fight my battles victoriously.

In the scriptures, David said to the Philistine, "You come to me with a sword, with a spear, and with a javelin. But I come to You in the name of the Lord of Hosts, the God of the armies of Israel, whom You have defiled" (1 Sam. 17:45, NIV).

Jehovah Sabaoth, I am grateful that You are always standing in the gap for me, interceding on my behalf with Your powerful sword that causes trouble to melt and be still amid Your presence. I magnify Your name and am in awe of Your strength that You show each day on my behalf. I pray that You give me the wisdom to know how to position myself as You manifest the victories in my life, both small and great. You are indeed the Lord of armies.

Entry Two

Isaiah 63:3 (KJV) says, "Holy, holy, holy is the Lord of Hosts; the whole earth is full of his glory." I am appreciative of who You are, Your mighty hand, Your authority, Your victory, and Your purpose for Your children.

I am reminded of a dear friend who lived an active life; she was happy and loved and served the Lord with much praise and honor. Satan was extremely angry and wanted to steal her glory, ripping the very essence of joy from her spirit, her soul, leaving her paralyzed on one side of her body. No doubt, this left her overwhelmed and powerless amid her present circumstance. However, the Lord of Hosts stepped in and became her strong tower as she cried out to Him for hope, deliverance, and peace. I watched the empowerment of God manifest His strength amid her condition. Through the influence of God, she began to transform her attitude and outlook on life, knowing that God had a greater purpose in the making.

Each time I went to the nursing home to see her, she was always in good spirits and had a positive outlook on life despite what was before her. She began to suit up with the whole armor of God to do battle and take back what was taken from her. Under the unction of the Holy Spirit, she fastened her belt of truth, put on her breastplate of righteousness, feet shod with the gospel of peace, shield of faith, helmet of salvation, and the sword of the Spirit. Having those weapons working for her, victory was already won.

She started a ministry in the nursing home, sharing the Word of God with others to give them hope for the future. Her first goal was to leave the nursing home and get an apartment of her own. She began working relentlessly during her physical therapy, calling agencies for future assistance for housing and other needs to help her with sustainability as she transitioned from the nursing home back into society.

Finally, her blessing came, she was able to set up her apartment, received medical care assistance, and was grateful to God for all he had done in her life. "The name of the Lord is a strong tower; the righteous runs into it and is safe" (Prov. 18:10, KJV).

To the great and mighty God, my cup runs over with much gratitude that You were available to her, fighting her battles, protecting her from the wiles of the devil. He may have touched her physically, but I am grateful that You did not allow Satan to steal her soul. Thank You for giving her joy, and hope for the future.

Entry Three

When tragedy prowls at our door, hindering us from living an abundant life, it sometimes leaves us bitter and broken. When faced with these feelings, I am filled with gratitude that Jehovah Sabaoth is powerful when we are powerless and is there for us in times of trouble. James 4:2 (NIV) says, "You have not because you ask not."

Our job is to go to God, tell him all about our problems, failures, and inadequacies and he will hear our cry. When we go to the Lord of Hosts, we will not walk away the same. In the book of 1 Samuel, I'm reminded of Hannah who was barren and could not have children. She tried for years and years to become impregnated but to no avail; she remained infertile, leaving her with a broken heart. Amid her damaged heart, she cried out to the Lord of Hosts.

When God manifested himself to her, it transformed her whole attitude. While God did not grant her the son that she wanted at that time, she walked away radiant with a peaceful spirit that surpasses all understanding. Thank You, God, for being the first and last, a God that stands beside us in all things, giving us strength to walk through disappointments and tough times.

"For the LORD of hosts will have a day of reckoning Against everyone who is proud and lofty And against everyone who is lifted up, That he may be abased." Isaiah 2:12 (ESV)

Day 17

Friday, September 17, 2021

Jehovah-Shammah: The Lord That Is Always Present

Entry One

J ehovah Shammah, I lift You with the highest praise for You are worthy. Thank You for being present in my life and walking with me daily in every situation. Despite my shortcomings, You continue to show Your abiding presence in my life, loving me with unconditional love.

Your promising Word tells me, "Be strong and courageous. Do not be afraid or terrified because of them, for the Lord Your God goes with You; he will never leave You nor forsake You" (Deut. 31:6, NIV).

These words are so comforting to me and assure me of Your love and protection over me regardless of my past. I am grateful that even amid my mess-ups, You provide an opportunity for me to repent of my sins and get it right with You. Your presence, love, and unwavering compassion for me are truly appreciated. I can count on You to stand by my side when everyone else may abandon me.

Entry Two

Father God, thank You for always being present in my life and attentive to my needs. Growing up as a teenager, I felt isolated, ridiculed, and cast out in my neighborhood. Living in the projects already had its drawbacks and on top of that, I was treated like a second-class citizen, making me feel like I didn't belong, a misfit. I was so tired of people calling me an Oreo, suggesting that I'm black on the outside but white on the inside. My mother often told me that they were jealous because I was trying to make something out of myself. The devil didn't want me to do good or prosper. He desired to keep me in bondage by enslaving others to do unkind deeds and gestures unto me.

The only thing that kept me sane was my relationship with God and holding on to the fact that He loved me no matter what. During my lonely hours, Jehovah Shammah was always there comforting, loving, and guiding me, giving me the strength to persevere through difficult times.

I am grateful for Your Word that reminds me, "The LORD also will be a stronghold for the oppressed, A stronghold in times of trouble; And those who know Your name will put their trust in You, For You, O LORD, have not forsaken those who seek You" (Ps. 9:9-10, ESV).

Lord, I put my trust in You for You have never failed me. Thank You for blessing my life over the years. You deserve all the admiration and praise for all that You have done in my life.

Entry Three

When I think about Jehovah Shammah, the Lord that is always present in the life of His people, I think about Moses and his relationship with God. God believed in Moses even when he didn't believe in himself. Moses used every excuse possible for why he couldn't be a leader, a mouthpiece for God to use to help the Israelites.

God tells us to, "Trust in the Lord with all your heart and lean not on your own understanding; in all your ways submit to him, and he will make your paths straight" (Prov. 3:5-6, NIV).

God assured Moses that he would be with Him; his job was to be obedient. As such, Jehovah Shammah was with Moses when he led 600,000 people out of Egypt in the middle of the night; making sure they did not go through the land of enemies. He was with Moses when the Red Sea was parted so that they could cross over to safe land. He provided a pillar of clouds during the day and a pillar of fire during the night to ensure that they knew the direction in which to journey.

While so much more happened in the life of Moses and the Israelites, this is a glimpse of how God reminded them that He was with them every step of the way as they sought to reach the Promised Land. Likewise, God has always had his hand on my life from my childhood up to now, knowingly and unknowingly. I thank God for the Moseses of the world that gives us a gentle reminder of how awesome our God is and the length He will go to protect us and keep us safe as we face trials and tribulations in our lives.

"The LORD your God is with you, the Mighty Warrior who saves. He will take great delight in you; in his love he will no longer rebuke you, but will rejoice over you with singing." Zephaniah 3:17 (NIV)

Saturday, September 18, 2021

Jehovah-Machsi: You Are My Dwelling Place

Entry One

J ehovah-Machsi, You are my dwelling place, shelter in a time of need. I give genuine thanks to You for covering me in the blood of Jesus, commanding Your angels to guard over me from the evils of this world. Father God, "You are my strength and my fortress, my refuge in time of distress" (Jer. 16:19, NIV).

I'm reminded when I was a little girl; I would always beg my mother to let me go with her to evening church services. In my mind for some reason, it was a place of love and protection. This was my safety zone from all of the chaos that was going on at home. My daddy always found a reason to physically abuse my mother. When we would come home from church, he would accuse her of having a cologne scent on her, insinuating that she was with a man, and the list goes on and on. While I didn't truly know God at such a young age, as I look back over my life, yet again, he guarded my mind and protected me from sheer insanity. I am a living testimony that God had a hedge of thorns of protection around me, keeping me safe for such a time as this. As I write this gratitude journal, it is the will of God that I share my thoughts with others that they will be blessed as they reflect on the goodness of God in their lives. I thank You Jehovah-Machsi for Your tender, loving arms that hold Your children so tightly, making us know that we are indeed safe in You. What a mighty God we serve.

Entry Two

My best friend has been a constant blessing in my life. With her unwavering faith in God, she encourages me to give up my best and trust the Lord in all things. Despite any hardships she faces in her life, the first name she calls on is "Jesus," followed by running straight into the arms of God for protection and guidance. I remember when she was diagnosed with stage 4 cancer; she could have easily given up and embraced cancer in her life, awaiting her death. Instead, she chose to seek God who is her refuge and fortress in a time of need. God tells us, "Trust in him at all times, O people; pour out your heart before him; God is a refuge for us. Selah" (Psalm 62:8, ESV).

Because of her faith in God, applying his Word to her life, and seeking His face energetically, God healed her body. Jehovah Machsi, I thank you for sending friends in my life that are an encouragement to help me preserve until the day You return for me. Knowing that You are my strength amid hardships gives me hope for a brighter tomorrow.

Entry Three

As I look at what is presently happening in the world, I can see that we are truly living in the last days. COVID has claimed millions of lives and continues to run rampant, seeking who it can devour; mob attacks on the United States Capitol creates chaos and division in the world, people are randomly being shot for no apparent reason, mothers are against daughters, fathers are against sons, and the insurmountable list continues.

Even amid what is going on around, we can be encouraged by God's Word that says, "Let us then with confidence draw near to the throne of grace, that we may receive mercy and find grace to help in time of need" (Heb. 4:16, ESV).

As we go before the Lord, we must position ourselves to hear Him, wait on Him for He will strengthen us to stand against the wiles of the devil. Thank You, Jehovah Machsi, for being my haven, a place of protection during the ups and downs of life's experiences. You are the light of the world; my exclusive spiritual light embodied with steadfast truths. It is through the illuminating light of Your Word that transfers me from darkness into the heavenly brightness of God. Help me to always let my light shine that others will see the renewing of my mind and the transformation of ways, glorifying You in all things.

"Because thou hast made the Lord, which is my refuge, even the most High, thy habitation; There shall no evil befall thee, neither shall any plague come nigh thy dwelling." Psalm 91:9-10 (KJV)

Day 19

Sunday, September 19, 2021

El Roi: The God Who Sees Me

Entry One

L iving in a diversified society creates a lot of dynamics in your life. There are times when I feel misunderstood, invisible, and unheard, but I am grateful that I serve a God who knows everything about me; he hears me, he sees me, and he watches over me. What is even more fascinating is that He knows the number of hairs that are on my head. Amid trillions and trillions of people in the world, He distinctively knows my voice from anyone else. That's too much for my little finite mind to comprehend.

As such, I lift up El Roi, the God who sees me when no one else can identify with my struggles, my plight. When I look around me and see all of the many blessings that happen to me daily, I know that El Roi has not forgotten me. Having the assurance of God is a blessed gift in my life. When I face hard times, I look to Him for renewed hope, stirring me up to press forward to see what the end will be. I am grateful to God for helping me to understand that every bit of my sufferings or misfortunes are there to fulfill his heavenly purpose for my life.

God said, "The eyes of the LORD are on the righteous, and his ears are attentive to their cry" (Ps. 34:15).

Because I belong to You, El Roi, I am deemed righteous and have a special place in Your heart. Thank You, God, for hearing my cry when I call out Your name. You never slumber or sleep and are faithful and committed to keeping me safe. To the One who sees me, I put all my trust and faith in You to protect, guard, and deliver me from the whirlwinds of this world. What an incredible, wonderful, and superlative God I serve.

Entry Two

A few years ago, I met a young lady that struggled with her husband being sent to prison for many years because he inappropriately touched a teenager. After much prayer with God, she decided to stay in the marriage and honor her marriage vows. A great deal of her family members distanced themselves from her, gossiping and saying all kinds of unpleasant things about her, feeling that she should have left him and moved on with her life. During this time, she felt abandoned, invisible, and misunderstood by others. Nevertheless, she refused to stay in the seat of pity and depression. She stayed before the Lord, praying because she knew El Roi knew her better than she knew herself.

The Word of God says, "I am the good shepherd. I know my own and my own know me, just as the Father knows me and I know the Father; and I lay down my life for the sheep" (John 10:14-15, ESV).

God saw her amid all her brokenness, pain, abandonment, and shame. The more the Holy Spirit ministered to her needs, the stronger and more confident she became. She is now back with her husband and both of them are living a life for Christ. Thank You, El Roi, for seeing the dark moments in our lives and reaching way down to pick us up out of the muck and marrow, setting us on a new path.

Entry Three

In the book of Genesis, beginning in Chapter 11, I am reminded of Hagar, an Egyptian female servant of Abraham and Sarah. She didn't have anyone who tried to know her and truly see her. I'm sure she felt invisible and insignificant to people. Her life was a sheer chain reaction, transitioning from one person to the next. Pharaoh gave her to Abraham. From there she became a servant to Sarah, and Sarah gave her to Abraham as a wife. The saga gets increasingly worse when there was a controversy between Sarah and Hagar when she became impregnated with a child from Abraham. Although Hagar was carrying a child from Abraham, he didn't stand up for her but gave her up as well. Can you imagine being an object of what someone else wants with little or no regard for your feelings? Hagar was a part of a family that knew God, but it turned out that Abraham and Sarah became flawed believers in the eyes of Hagar. This caused her to flee from Sarah and Abraham and in turn, she ran from God.

Scripture tells us, "The angel of the Lord found her by a spring of water in the wilderness, the spring on the way to Shur" (Gen. 16:7, ESV).

God has a way of stepping into our lives right on time, even while being angry and resentful. He saw her affliction and her pain, walking beside her even when she was unaware. God told Hagar to return to her mistress with submission. God also told her that he would multiply her offspring. While it isn't certain that Hagar ever prayed unto God, we know that God listens to our affliction and hears our tears, for they are unspoken Words that only He understands. Heavenly Father, I am grateful that You gave her a heart to eventually cry out to You, acknowledging that You were looking after her. Thank You for Your grace that is sufficient enough for all the other Hagars of this world. It is these kinds of stories in the Bible, which reinforce the gratefulness of who You are in our lives. With much gratitude, I exalt You to the highest for knowing Your children and giving us what we need in Your time and season.

"This is the confidence we have in approaching God: that if we ask any-thing according to his will, he hears us." 1 John 5:14 (NIV)

Day 20

Monday, September 20, 2021

El Olam: The Eternal and Everlasting God

Entry One

F ather God, I seek to know who You truly are and the many wonders that only You can perform. You are El Olam, the eternal and everlasting God, the first and the last for there is none like You. It is declared that You are the true and living God, every knee will bow down before You and all will confess that You are Lord.

Scripture declares that we must, "Trust in the Lord forever, for the Lord God is an everlasting rock" (Isa. 42:4, ESV).

I am grateful to You for being the everlasting rock that I can depend on at all times. When I'm weak, You are my strength, the everlasting arm on which I can lean. When I look around me, I can see that this world is constantly changing as well as the people of the world, but the one thing that I can count on is that You are always the same and consistent in all You do. Thank You for all ways being available, loving, and full of grace and mercy.

Entry Two

In Genesis 21:33 (NIV), the Word of God tells, "And Abraham planted a grove in Beersheba, and called there on the name of the LORD, the everlasting (Olam) God (El)." I submit all thanks to You, the forever present and everlasting God. Your existence is perplexing for mere words can't describe the awesomeness of Your glory. Your greatness is infinite, self-sufficient, and eternal. Father God, You are my eternal haven. I desire to seek after You with all my heart as a token of my appreciation for your many blessings in my life. You are my counsel amid troublesome situations in my life.

Growing up, I was very concerned about the large consumption of alcohol and drugs among some of my family members. I watched the drinking of alcohol strip away dignity, self-worth, destroy relationships, leaving a feeling of desolation. Through intercessory prayer, I could see God's mercy and love as He touched each generation, blessing them and giving them a greater purpose for living. Many of them now have surrendered their lives unto God, giving Him glory and praise for all things. While I continue to see some remnants of this generational curse attempting to raise its ugly head, I am both grateful and confident that my eternal God, who knows all and sees all, will deliver, for He has a time and season for all things.

"Now unto him that is able to keep you from falling, and to present you faultless before the presence of his glory with exceeding joy, to the only wise God our Saviour, be glory and majesty, dominion and power, both now and ever. Amen" (Jude 1:24-25 KJV).

Entry Three

Almighty God, You are the everlasting One who has been available to all of Your people throughout the ages. After Your creation, You saw that it was all good; then You made man in the likeness of Your image and breathed the breath of life into him, and it was good. As the God of time without end, You blessed Adam and Eve abundantly in the garden of Eden but asked them not to eat from the tree of knowledge. Nevertheless, their curiosity and disobedience took shape and they ignored the command of God, resulting in a curse that transfers to all mankind. With that being said, El Olam is the same God that was with Adam and Eve at the beginning of time and continues to be the same God in our contemporary society. Heavenly Father, I am grateful that Your Word instructs us in plain terms of Your expectations of Godly living as well as the consequences for disobedience.

"Hast thou not known? Hast thou not heard that the everlasting God, the Lord, the Creator of the ends of the earth, fainteth not, neither is weary? There is no searching of his understanding" (Isa. 40:28, KJV).

Just as Adam and Eve received their judgment for disobeying, both the righteous and the unrighteous will be judged in the end for it does not matter what era we live in. God occupies every space in the universe at all times and is the same yesterday, today, and in the future, consistent in all things. The question becomes, will we live eternity with El Olam or in hell for all eternity? I am grateful to my eternal God for making it possible for all to have a chance to live with Him in the new heaven and the earth for all eternity with our endless God.

"The eternal God is your refuge, and underneath are the everlasting arms. He will drive out your enemies before you, saying, 'Destroy them!'"
Deuteronomy 33:27 (NIV)

Day 21

Tuesday, September 21, 2021

Jehovah-Melech Olam: The Lord and King Forever

Entry One

It is a privilege and honor to serve a God who forever reigns over all the heavens and the earth. I come before You, Jehovah-Melech Olam, acknowledging You as the King forever, the Lord over my life and every living creature and being here on earth. The Word of God confirms this in Psalms 10:16 (KJV), when it says, "The LORD is King forever and ever (Melech 'Olam): the heathen are perished out of His land."

I am grateful to God that I don't have to be afraid now or in the future because I serve a God who rules over all. The Word tells me that He will save the faithful, humble, and righteous, but the oppressors will be punished. When mankind comes up against me, I don't have to feel desperate because I know that I am protected by the eternal God who resides forevermore.

However, there are times when I let the enemy get the best of me by attempting to fight my own battles. When that happens, I thank God for the Holy Spirit that reminds me that the battle is not mine, it is the Lord's. With an overflowing of gratitude, I am blessed that - Jehovah Melech-Olam - lives and reigns to help me now and, in the future.

Entry Two

God has given us a promise that cannot be revoked for He has declared that He is King from eternity to eternity. Through the blood of Jesus, God's oath has been established. With that being said, there is nothing that Satan can do to change what God has put into place. Father God, I am grateful that Your Word is abiding and will never return unto me void, and I thank You for Your shield of protection, guidance, and deliverance.

God's Word says, "But you are a chosen generation, a royal priesthood, a holy nation, His own special people, that you may proclaim the praises of Him who called you out of darkness into His marvelous light" (1 Pet. 2:9, KJV).

Wow, I am the daughter of the King of the universe; life doesn't get any better than that. As I was growing up, I had ambitious plans for my life, goals that I wanted to attain, things I wanted to do, and places I wanted to go. Over the years, God has blessed my life with insurmountable blessings and sometimes I want to pinch myself to see if I am living this life or dreaming. As I grew older and wiser, I realized that the things of this world are temporal and will pass away for only the things of God will last for all eternity.

My eternal God walked into my life and introduced me to what true living is all about. The day that I decided to relinquish my life unto God was the best decision that I could have ever made. I may not be rich with money, but I am royalty through my God of the universe. Making God Lordship over my life shifted my thinking to things that are eternal and lasting. I now live a life with heavenly benefits of freedom of choice, provision of unconditional love from God, the forgiveness of sins, a new creature in Christ Jesus, and so much more. This meant that I could no longer operate from the world's point of view but look to God's instruction for my life.

While it is OK to have material possessions, those possessions should not define who you are for they can become idols that easily separate us from the eternal God who governs the universe. Thank You, Jehovah-Melech Olam, for being a God of all seasons now and at all times.

Entry Three

Our Father, which art in heaven, how holy, consecrated, and sacred is Your name. I chose to focus on the greatness and glory of who You are in my life. Your name is set apart from all names because thou art God and beside thee, there is no other. Your awesome wisdom and glory are infinite, and I worship and praise Your name with the highest exaltation for You have been my wheel in the middle of the wheel, my bright and shining star, help when I'm in trouble, a lawyer in my defense, and countless other ways You show up in my life.

Ephesians 1:3 (NIV) states, "Praise be to the God and Father of our Lord Jesus Christ, who has blessed us in the heavenly realms with every spiritual blessing in Christ."

I count it a blessing that You look beyond my faults and see my needs rendering an overflow of blessings in my life. The question becomes, who wouldn't want to serve a God like You who spills over with grace and mercy? While there may be times that we experience headaches and heartaches that may cause us to doubt God, but when we think of the goodness of Your mercy and grace, it changes the atmosphere. Only the true and living God, the God of eternity, the everlasting God, the King of kings, and the Prince of Peace can make that kind of divine shift in our lives.

Jehovah-Melech Olam, my Lord and King, forever loves me and continues to work in the background for my good. I'm reminded of Noah in the book of Genesis who was righteous, faithful, and loved the Lord. God was disappointed that the people were running rampant with wickedness and evil in their hearts that God wanted to annihilate the world, but found a remnant in Noah and his family and saved them from destruction. Now that's grace, and He continues to show the same grace for His people today, our everlasting King of kings, for He forever reigns.

"I am the Alpha and the Omega," says the Lord God, "who is and who was and who is to come, the Almighty." Revelations 1:8 (NIV)

Day 22

Wednesday, September 22, 2021

Jehovah-Sel'i: Rock of My Salvation

Entry One

Jehovah Sel'i, I come before You this day, thanking You for being the rock of my salvation. You are the basis for my hope, my confidence, my redeemer, and deliverance as I face today and tomorrow. I pledge to rejoice in You, be patient amid tribulation, and walk a life of faith in You and Your Word because You are my strength, my shield, the horn of my salvation, my stronghold, refuge, and Savior. I delight in You, the Most High God, my Redeemer.

Exodus 15:2 (NLT) tells me that, "The Lord is my strength and my song; he has given me victory. This is my God, and I will praise him—my father's God, and I will exalt him!"

All praises unto God for giving Bill Gaither the mind to write the song "Because He Lives" that says, "Because He lives, I can face tomorrow, because He lives all fear is gone, because I know He holds the future, and life is worth the living just because He lives." This song speaks to my spirit and my exaltation to the Lord who holds a victory over life and death. The security that God gives me, and the reminder that He is my strong tower, give me the courage and the calm assurance to face all uncertainties in my life. My God is an awesome God, my rock from everlasting to everlasting.

Entry Two

I come before You God, the rock of all times, elevating me with Your strength to continue to run the race of living a godly life until the end of time. Even amid my shortcomings, You have blessed me beyond measure. I am grateful, heavenly Father for my sons and grandchildren that You have given me. It is a blessing that I am able to be a living witness of a new generation and hopefully a part of the new generation to come. This, I do not take lightly because many desired to be a part of such a time as this, but have gone on to their destination beyond this world and will never have the opportunity to partake in such a special moment in time.

Your Word declares, "I will establish My covenant between Me and you and your descendants after you throughout their generations as an everlasting covenant, to be God to you and to your descendants after you" (Gen. 17:7, NIV).

With an outburst of gratitude, thank You, Jehovah-Sel'i, for Your promise to watch over my family from generation to generation, to protect them, and be their security in a time of need. I intercede in prayer that they will receive and love You as their Lord and Savior in all things, developing an intimate relationship with You, trusting and rendering praise unto You, the rock of their salvation.

I am grateful that You are the solid foundation and role model for them to build a life that conforms to be more like Jesus each day. Help my family to respect Your authority as Lord even amid a contemporary society attempting to pull them down with the strongholds of worldly pleasures that so easily beset them. Oh Great Jehovah, I am grateful unto You for being my protector, my savior, and my power. I humbly ask You to cover my family in the blood of Jesus and break down every stronghold in their lives, delivering them in the precious name of Jesus.

Scripture says, "Behold, I have given you authority to tread on serpents and scorpions, and over all the power of the enemy, and nothing shall hurt you" (Luke 10:19, ESV).

Entry Three

Father God, I bow before You, thank You for being forever present in my life. As I travel this life, I build my faith on nothing less than my Savior's blood and righteousness. Where everything else in this world is temporary, I can look to You for a dwelling place for all eternity. Thank You for Your amazing grace. Jehovah Sel'i, You are perfect in all Your ways, a refuge for Your children, the light of the world, a strong force to be reckoned with, and hope forever and a day.

The Word of God says, "I am the vine; you are the branches. Whoever abides in me and I in him, he it is that bears much fruit, for apart from me you can do nothing" (John 15:5, ESV).

This divine Word tells me that when I became a new creature in Christ Jesus, I became a child of God. This gave me the ticket to be a branch on God's vine. With that being said, the fruits of the Spirit in my life connect me to God and the resources needed to be victorious over all attacks from Satan and his followers. In short, the Word of God informs me that I can do all things by His strength if I believe and trust Him as my rock. Jehovah-Sel'i, my trust is in You, and if I falter, bring Your Word back to my remembrance, convict my mind, accept my repentant heart, and set me back on the right path.

"No one is holy like the Lord! There is no one besides You; there is no Rock like our God." 1 Samuel 2:2 (NIV)

Day 23

Thursday, September 23, 2021

Jehovah-Go'el: My Redeemer

Entry One

Oh Great Jehovah, thank You for covering me with Your blessings every day of my life. Today, I have a song of praise in my spirit, "I Just Want to Thank You Lord," by Lynda Randle and Angela Primm that says, "Thank You, Lord. You've been so good, You saved my soul, I just want to thank You Lord." Heavenly Father, You are Jehovah-Go'el, my redeemer, setting me free from the bondage of sin and all other strongholds that became captives in my life.

I humbly come before You, acknowledging that I am nothing without You for my life is extensionally meaningless; I need You in my life. I am filled with gratitude that You saw that I was hell bound and You stepped in freely giving up Your life as ransom, paying the price for my sins through Your death on the cross. Words can't begin to explain how grateful I am for forgiveness and Your blood that was shed on the cross so that I can have eternal life.

The Word of God says, "Therefore, there is now no condemnation for those who are in Christ Jesus, because through Christ Jesus the law of the Spirit who gives life has set you free from the law of sin and death" (Rom. 8:1-2, NIV).

God, Your Word tells me that I am no longer a prisoner to sin and death because I am in Christ Jesus. I am grateful, Jehovah Go'el, that I am under the dispensation of grace and mercy for under the law, I would not have had a fighting chance. You are my redeemer.

Entry Two

Growing up with eight children in the family can have its good times as well as difficulties. Looking on the downside, I can remember how each one of us would get in trouble with our devilish ways and refused to own up to what we had done. As I reminisce on my childhood, I remember my mother calling all of us into the house to find out who took her money off of the dresser. Each one of us would put on our innocent faces and continue to cry crocodile tears, but that didn't stop my mother from beating our behinds.

My mother would go down the line whipping each one of us until one of us confessed that we took the money. As a child, I was angry, upset, and outraged for being whipped for something I did not do. But when we take this idea and look through the spiritual lens of Jesus, a God that is fully man and fully God who had no sin, did no wrong, was holy, righteous, faithful, merciful, and so much more was sacrificed as ransom for our sins. Yes, God gave up His best for an undeserving sinner like me. Jesus was beaten until he was not recognizable, spit on, cursed, called every name but a child of God, followed by hanging Him on the cross to pay the debt of sin. He was innocent and should have been angry, upset, and outraged, but He willingly accepted the punishment out of agape love for me, and by His redeeming blood, the gift of salvation was at hand.

The scripture declares, "Knowing that you were not redeemed with corruptible things, like silver or gold, from your aimless conduct received by tradition from your fathers, but with the precious blood of Christ, as of a lamb without blemish and without spot" (1 Pet. 18-19, NKJV).

Jehovah Go'el, I am truly grateful to You for Your uncondi-tional love for me and the sacrifice You so freely made so that the chains that had me bound in sin could be broken, giving me the freedom to enter into the realm of God for all eternity.

Entry Three

About ten or more years ago, I met a young lady who was very distraught because she felt that her entire marriage was based on a lie. When she met her husband, in her mind, she felt that he adored her for he was very attentive to her needs. However, he had a dark side in his life. There is an old saying, "What's done in the dark, will come into the light." One night, he was out drinking and was stopped by the police because he was weaving on the roads. The police officers informed her husband that he would have to call someone to pick up the car or they would have it impounded. Needless to say, the young lady got the phone call to come and pick up the car. When she got to the scene, the policeman told her that there was more to the story for her hus-band had a prostitute in the car with him. As she shared her story with me, I could see the depth of pain, agony, rage, brokenness, and sorrow that overtook her body, mind, and soul for her world was shattered.

I am grateful that she knew God and trusted Him to give her the direction she needed to overcome such a tragic moment in her life. This kind of faith gave me hope and the determination to approach God with the same kind of commitment and dedication as I walk through the valley and shadows of calamities in my life. Instead of me ministering to her, she ministered to the core of my heart, invoking a deeper desire to draw closer to God. If He could mend her wounds in such a time as this, the sky is the limit to what He will do for all who are faithful to Him and His Word.

God reveals, "I waited patiently for the Lord; he turned to me and heard my cry. He lifted me out of the slimy pit, out of the mud and mire; he set my feet on a rock and gave me a firm place to stand. He put a new song in my mouth, a hymn of praise to our

God. Many will see and fear the Lord and put their trust in him" (Ps. 40:1-3, NIV).

She knew that no earthly counselor, man, or woman could deliver her from her present state of mind. In her darkest hour, she basked in the presence of the Lord, growing stronger and stronger each day through His Word that gave her hope and fulfillment. He was her strength, her rock, and her redeemer. Jehovah Go'el, I am grateful that You surrounded this young woman with love, mercy, comfort, and strength through her suffering. Thank You for restoring her faith, giving her hope for the future, and the assurance of knowing that You are with her always, even until the end of this world. I am grateful that You send people into my life with God inspiring stories that are shared as testimonies to others who are having trouble in their marriages. Through Your redeeming blood, we have the victory over all things.

> *"Let the words of my mouth and the meditation of my heart be acceptable in Your sight, O Lord, my rock and my redeemer." Psalms 19:14 (ESV)*

Day 24

Friday, September 24, 2021

Jehovah-'Ori: The Lord My Light

Entry One

When I think about the word light, it brings to mind something visible, bright, illuminating one's path, and makes it possible for one to see. Transferring this to the spiritual eye, light becomes profound because it is one of the many characteristics of the God I serve. There is safety and assurance in the Godly light that engulfs me, giving me the spiritual vision to see the things that are unseen with the carnal eye.

The Word of God states, "I am the light of the world. Whoever follows me will never walk in darkness but have the light of life," (John 8:12, NIV).

Jehovah-'Ori, You are my God of light and because of You, I will not have to walk in the path of darkness. I am grateful that You are life and through You, I am granted eternal life. You came to this dying world as an eternal, shining light, giving us the gift of salvation. I will never take Your love and sacrifice for granted for that is why I praise and worship You, the only wise God and Savior, both now and forever. Heavenly Father, I pray that You use me as a vessel to live a life that is reflective of Your Son, Jesus, the perfect model that You sent for me as a reflection of what my life should be.

Help me, Jehovah-'Ori, to show the love of Christ shining through me that others will see Your work in my life and glorify You who are in the heavens. While there have been and will be dark moments in my life, I can walk through them without fear, knowing that You are my light, my God, my rock, my strength, and my salvation. It is in You who I put my trust for Your Word is built on a solid foundation and will never crumble.

Entry Two

Heavenly Father, You have given me a life of goodness, fulfillment, victory, and peace in knowing that You are always shining on the pathway of my life. Psalms 27:1 (NIV) tells us, "The LORD is my light and my salvation— whom shall, I fear? The LORD is the stronghold of my life— of whom shall I be afraid?"

If God is light and peace, then Satan is darkness and chaos seeking to plant fear in the lives of God's people. Thank You, Jehovah-'Ori, for always reminding me that when fear comes in my life, it is a device from Satan to destroy me, removing me from Your light. I remember when I found out that I was pregnant with my eldest son, a flood of fear came over me planting doubt in my mind. This shook my confidence, and I started to question if I had what it took to be a mother. I went into somewhat of a depressive state, internalizing my fears so that I would not be looked upon as inadequate.

Satan took something that was supposed to be the light of my world and turned it into a dark place in my life. My spirit of discernment surfaced, recognizing the works of the devil and his plan to steal my moment of glory. As such, the Holy Spirit began to speak to me, informing me that Satan was using the hardships and afflictions of my past experiences as a young girl and brought them into my adulthood, using it as a tactic or stronghold to keep me from enjoying the life that God intended for me.

Nehemiah 8:10 (ESV) declares, "And do not be grieved, for the joy of the LORD is your strength."

My heavenly Father brought me out of the darkness and back into the light allowing me to enjoy the process of my pregnancy and all the love I had to give my son. I am eternally grateful that I have a relationship with God and it was through His Word and strength that I was able to rebuke Satan and his attempt to use my past as bait to steal my future. Praise and glory to the Highest God that continues to be the light of my world (Jehovah- 'Ori). Because I am safeguarded in Him, Satan has no chance of stealing my joy.

Entry Three

Jehovah 'Ori, You are the Lord of my life. I am grateful that Your Word is, "A lamp unto feet and a light unto my path" (Ps. 119:105, KJV).

Without Your presence and the guidance of Your illuminating Word that governs my behavior, I would be a fallen sheep, hell-bound. Because of Your goodness, love, grace, and mercy, I am delivered, and I'm able to walk with confidence in the plan that you have tailored just for me. I'm elated that you are that strong beacon of light that brightens my way of life.

When I think about light, I can't help but think about darkness. While I'm not afraid of the dark, there is something mystic and unsettling about darkness in the absence of light. The idea of not being able to see what is behind you, before you, or on the side of you, leaves me with an uneasy feeling, making me wonder what is lurking around the space I occupy.

Scripture tells us, "To open their eyes so that they may turn from darkness to light and from the dominion of Satan to God, that they may receive forgiveness of sins and an inheritance among those who have been sanctified by faith in Me" (Acts 26:18, KJV).

Thank you, oh gracious God, for turning on the light in my life so that my eyes opened, turning me away from the darkness that had me bound and pointing me in the direction of Jesus.

Moreover, I can remember times when we had power out-ages in the house; I would quickly scurry around the house to find candles to bring forth light so that I would be able to see where I was going and a clear path on how to get there. Likewise, because Jehovah- 'Ori is the light in my life that enlightens my path, I walk in the assurance of knowing that there is no hidden agenda in Him for all is exposed in His Word that tells me exactly what needs to be done to enter into His kingdom.

As such, I serve a God that is all-seeing, forever present, and knows all things. Therefore, I have no worries about Satan's acts of darkness because all his attempts are exposed by the light of God. I am grateful that Jehovah-'Ori's light will forever shine for there are no power outages that can stop the ray of sunshine from glowing in my life. Man's light may not be available when in need, but I know that God's light will always be present. Glory to the Most High God who shines on this world.

"Arise, shine; for your light has come, And the glory of the LORD has risen upon you." Isaiah 60:1 (NIV)

Day 25

Saturday, September 25, 2021

Jehovah-'Izuz 'Gibbor: Lord Who Is Strong and Mighty

Entry One

You are the Lord who is strong and mighty (Jehovah- 'Izuz 'Gibbor); the one who empowers and gives us strength to face oppositions in our lives. I know when difficulties come in my life; I can turn my back away from the negative and fix my eyes on the Great Counselor of all things. It is in You that I find peace and assurance that victory is at hand because I serve a God who is mighty above all that proclaim to be a god.

Thank You for teaching me how to use Your Word of truths to meditate on day and night. It is through Your Word, which creates metamorphosis in my thinking and being, living a life that is reflective of our Savior.

Jeremiah 10:6 (NIV) reminds me that, "No one is like You, O LORD. You are great, and Your Name is MIGHTY in power."

I exalt and reverence You in Your glory, strength, and power to save the lost through the redeeming blood of Jesus. So many people who don't know You in the pardon of their sins. Through a relationship with You and acknowledging Your Word, they will come to know Your strength and glorify the true and living God. Continue to empower me and other saints to go out into the vineyard and spread the good news of the Almighty One who has the power to save that which is lost.

Scripture proclaims, "Go into all the world and proclaim the gospel to the whole creation. Whoever believes and is baptized will be saved, but whoever does not believe will be condemned" (Mark 16:15-16, ESV).

Jehovah- 'Izuz Gibbor, I uplift You for You are indeed Lord of lords and King of kings, boundless, strong, and mighty in all things. You are the beacon of light in my life that keeps me going from day to day. I give You adoration, praise, and worship for your everlasting presence.

Entry Two

Hallelujah to the Highest, You are the Lord of my life, and I trust the plans that You have designed for me. I am grateful that You have given us the power of prayer to come before You during tough times, seeking Your strength to deliver us from a world of sin and adversities.

"Great is our Lord and mighty in power; His understanding has no limit" (Ps. 147:5, NIV).

There is nothing that we are not able to take to our Father in heaven. His ear is always fine-tuned to our needs and He makes us feel as if we are the only one with Him in the entire universe. How awesome it is to have a God that can tend to all of our individual needs while serving the entire world at the same time. To think about his vastness blows my mind. Jehovah- 'Izuz 'Gibbor, thank You for being my protector, my confidant, problem solver, and my strength to overcome life's adversities.

My friend and I had a deep conversation about marriage and how, with time, husbands and wives take the needs of each other for granted. We tend to often focus on the things that upset us the most or quirks that get on our nerves failing to emphasize the things that drew You to that person at the beginning of the relationship. The more we talked, the more convicted I felt for I was guilty of the crime. I mentioned earlier that I could take anything to God. So, I did, bearing all before His throne. My husband is one of the most thoughtful people I know, doing sweet little gestures to let me know He cares. After much talk with God, I was instructed to spend more time praying for my husband and acknowledging His goodness.

For the Word of God tells us to, "Confess your faults one to another, and pray one for another, that ye may be healed. The effectual fervent prayer of a righteous man availeth much" (James 5:6, KJV).

Instead of judging me, God redirected me to His Word. I am grateful to God Almighty for looking down on me with tender, loving compassion, giving me strength and empowerment to continue the race despite the hardships that come my way. I pledge to You, oh God, to make every attempt to look for the good in others, lift them, and not tear them down. If I fail, I thank you in advance for bringing it back to my remembrance.

Entry Three

I serve a God who is strong and mighty and is always ready to do battle for His children. I am so grateful that the love that my heavenly Father shows from day to day will never lose its power. While God's love is unconditional and is our source of strength in all things, we should not use it as an excuse to stagger in our weakness as if we are helpless creatures. If we are children of God, then we have a heritage of strength through him.

God tells us to, "Be strong, and let Your heart take courage, all you who wait for the LORD" (Ps. 31:24, ESV).

God made us and knew our limitations for He will not cast anything on us what we are unable to bear. As we face the many adversities that life throws at us, we have the power and strength to walk through with certainty because God has already given us the strength to be victorious. Help me to choose right over wrong despite the outcome.

To my Lord who is great and powerful, I thank You for giving me the strength to recognize my shortcomings, reminding me that I draw my strength from You through the legacy of Christ Jesus. As such, I ask You, oh Lord, to continue to do a work in me, giving me boldness and the strength to confront ungodliness and injustices using Your Word as a weapon to rightfully divide the truth.

"He will be called Wonderful Counselor, Mighty God, Everlasting Father, Prince of Peace."
Isaiah 9:6 (NIV)

Day 26

Sunday, September 26, 2021

Jehovah-Mephalti: The Lord My Deliverer

Entry One

Jehovah-Mephalti, You are my Lord, my deliverer, and I am grateful that You are continuously behind the scenes making intercessions for our good. Even in the beginning of time when man fell from the ark of Your safety in the garden of Eden, You had a divine plan in place to deliver us through the death of Jesus on the cross.

Scripture pronounces, "The LORD is my rock, and my fortress, and my deliverer; The God of my rock; in him will I trust: he is my shield, and the horn of my salvation, my high tower, and my refuge, my Saviour; thou savest me from violence" (2 Sam. 22:2-3, KJV).

While I know that we are filthy rags before You, not worthy of Your grace and mercy, I am appreciative of Your steadfast love that moved You to deliver us from this sin-sick world. When I think about my two sons, the very thought of giving up their lives for the atonement of sins of the world is inconceivable for no parent wants their son to die for any reason or purpose. Yet, God, with no hesitation, was willing to make that sacrificial offering, His only begotten Son to be the substitutional lamb for our sins.

The Word states, "For God did not send his Son into the world to condemn the world, but in order that the world might be saved through him" (John 3:17, ESV).

To an undeserving people, I can't thank my heavenly Father enough for swallowing up death, granting victory to us through our precious Savior, and deliverer, Jesus Christ. Your love is close to my heart, and I will guard it with top-notch security. Thank You, Jesus.

Entry Two

Father God, You are gracious, righteous, compassionate, and faithful to us in all things. Thank You so much for hearing our cries when the enemy comes against us, always listening and responding when we call.

Second Samuel 22:18 (ESV) states, "He rescued me from my strong enemy, from those who hated me, for they were too mighty for me."

While there are many stories in our Bible that speak of how God delivered His people out of the hands of their enemies, my mind goes straight to the deliverance of Moses and the Israelites from Pharaoh. God developed a great plan and orchestrated the life of Moses from childhood to adulthood, preparing him to be the called leader to lead the Israelites into freedom.

When Moses accepted his calling, God was able to work through Him using a strategic plan to overshadow the enemy to ensure that the people of God escaped the hands of the enemy. God is calling for a humble nation with a willing heart to listen and walk in the obedience of His Word. Father God, help me to position myself with a humble spirit to be used by You for the very purpose of serving Your people.

When I think back over my life, I can see Your hand in many ways, delivering me from sinful attacks from Satan. I am filled with gratitude that You have delivered me from emotional, sexual, and social abuse during the younger years of my life. Not only did You deliver me from the strongholds in my life but You restored me, shielded me, and protected me from the enemy, giving me a renewed life in You. I am grateful that I am a new creature in Christ, the old Rhonda has passed, and the newness of God lives through me. Praise, honor, and glory to my Lord and deliverer.

Entry Three

I serve a God that is our deliverer in so many ways. He heals us when we're sick physically or emotionally, gives us the power to conquer satanic forces that attack us, breaks strongholds that keep us down, gives us strength through suffering and so much more. Speaking of healing and suffering, our world needs healing and restoration as we face the tragedies of COVID-19 that have plagued our world.

If we have never found a need to turn to God, this is the perfect time to seek His face. Without Him, this world has no hope and no future, but with Him, there is deliverance and a brighter tomorrow. Hence, we must choose this day who we will serve and put our trust in the Almighty God for deliverance, certainly not the ways of the world.

Remember these comforting Words, "Even though I walk through the darkest valley, I will fear no evil, for You are with me; Your rod and Your staff, they comfort me" (Ps. 23:4, NIV).

This pandemic puts our world in a dark place that is deathly, filled with pain, agony, anger, disappointment, grief, among other emotions. While I know that countless people are in pain, I am grateful for the innumerable number of people that God has delivered for they forged through fire.

To the many families that have been touched by this pandemic, seek God's face for the deliverance of a broken and lonely heart. I am a living witness that Jehovah-Mephalti (my deliverer) will heal your broken hearts and make you whole again. Heavenly Father, as we move forward, give us a transformable attitude by seeking gratitude for the blessings that exist in our life.

"When the righteous cry for help, the Lord hears and delivers them out of all their troubles." Psalm 34:17 (KJV)

Day 27

Monday, September 27, 2021

Jehovah-Quanna: My God Is a Jealous God

Entry One

God is an exclusive God who refuses to compete with any other god of this universe. Hence, Jehovah-Quanna is a jealous God because He has invested so much in making it possible for us to have the gift of salvation and to reign with Him for eternity. God's jealousy comes from a place of love which is a contrast from the jealousy of the world; the two distinctions are incompatible which don't occupy the same space.

Scripture tells us, "No one can serve two masters; for either he will hate the one and love the other, or he will be devoted to one and despise the other. You cannot serve God and wealth" (Matt. 6:24, KJV).

I thank You, God, for Your Word that is sharper than a two-edged sword, discerning my thoughts and the intentions that I have in my heart. We are quick to say out loud that we will never allow anything to separate us from the love of God, but we spend less time seeking You and Your glory and more time doing the things of the world. I am grateful that God's Word keeps me in check, making me realize the hidden idols in my life that can easily manifest themselves into barriers that block my relationship with God. I thank You, Jehovah-Quanna, for Your desire that we all come to repentance and find completeness in You and You alone. It is our reasonable service to make a big deal about our God because He deserves it.

Entry Two

Jehovah Quanna deserves all of our worship, praise, and honor for he is the one that created all things, the sustainer of life, giver of salvation, protector of this world, healer when we are sick, and the list reaches into infinity. As such, it is obvious that no man far or near can scratch the surface of what God can do for His many wonders are incomprehensible. God will not receive our second best for He desires and demands our total worship and praise. We must choose this day to who we will give our allegiance – will it be God or Satan?

Exodus 20:5 (NASB) tells us, "You shall not worship them or serve them; for I, the Lord your God, am a jealous God, visiting the iniquity of the fathers on the children, on the third and the fourth generations of those who hate Me."

In the book of Daniel, Nebuchadnezzar made a huge, golden statue and told all the people when they heard the sound of the instruments everyone will bow down and worship His man-made god. The penalty for not bowing down to the golden statue would result in the person being thrown into the fiery furnace.

Three Hebrew boys, Shadrach, Meshach, and Abednego refused to bow down at this god that was created by man. Their faith and allegiance to worshiping the Most High God, Creator of the universe were not compromised even unto death. While they were thrown into the fiery furnace, God protected His children and delivered them from this dreadful and excruciating death sentence.

Jehovah Quanna, when I think about the Hebrew boys, it makes me appreciate the fact that I can serve the true and living God without being threatened or put to death. Even in this contemporary society, there are so many people in other countries who do not have the liberty of choosing to serve our Lord and Savior. They are living a life just as some believers in the biblical days, meeting privately in their homes to share their faith in fear of persecution of their belief in Christ Jesus. I hope and pray that we all will commit to praise and worship God as if it is your last time. We, the people of the United States of America, have so much to be thankful for.

Entry Three

God tells us in His Word, "You must worship no other gods, for the Lord, whose very name is Jealous, is a God who is jealous about his relationship with you" (Exod. 34:14, NLT).

We say with our Words that God is the center of our universe and we worship only Him. When You think about it, idols can be anything that you put before God whether it's knowing or unknowingly. Our security and fulfillment must be in God first and all other things are subservient to that.

God said in His Word for us not to let anything separate us from His love. Our society gets caught in attaining wealth, jewelry, designer clothes, sexual immorality, work, success, covetous, keeping up with the Joneses, obsessed with children, spouses, houses, and so forth. I am grateful that the Word of God warns me about these idolistic pleasures that build a wall between God and me, suffocating the life that connects me to God.

Father, this moves me to give myself a self-inventory of where I am in this process. Search me, Lord, if You find anything in my life that remotely looks like an idol, convict my mind and heart that I will turn away from it and turn toward You, the God of unconditional love. I am thankful for all the materialistic things You have blessed me with over the years, but I refuse to bow down and worship those things. I desire You to find favor in me and not the wrath of Your judgment.

I am the Lord; that is my name; my glory I give to no other, nor my praise to carved idols." Isaiah 42:8 (ESV)

Day 28

Tuesday, September 28, 2021

Alpha and Omega: I am The Beginning and The End

Entry One

You are Alpha and Omega, the beginning and the end, for there is no deity that compares to God Almighty for Your presence transcends eternity. You are all-sufficient in every way possible for You are the One who is, who was, and who is to come. When I think about the Alpha and Omega, I think about the creation.

Genesis 1:1-3 (NASB 1995) informs us, "In the beginning God created the heavens and the earth. The earth was formless and void, and darkness was over the surface of the deep, and the Spirit of God was moving over the surface of the waters. Then God said, 'Let there be light;' and there was light."

The story ends with the creation of man that was made in the image of God. Heavenly Father, without Your creation at the beginning of time, there would be no world, no me, and no people in existence. Just typing these words makes me cringe to think about life without you in. You are the only One who can bring meaning to a meaningless world.

I am grateful that You took the time to carefully form a world for me to enjoy the things You have put into place. Thank You for allowing me to be an heir of Your throne through the precious gift of salvation. Even before I was conceived in my mother's womb, You knew everything about me, the good, the bad, and the ugly; yet You saw me before You saw my condition. Thank You for Your tender loving compassion and capacity to look beyond my transgressions and see that I needed a Savior. My worship, praise, and honor to You come from the heart.

Entry Two

Revelation 22:13 (ESV) says, "I am the Alpha and the Omega, the first and the last, the beginning and the end."

I exalt the God who existed even before the creation. There will be no one before or no one after Him. Everyone in the entire universe will recognize the awesome glory, power, and might of who God is.

This is affirmed in Philippians 2:10-11 (NIV) when it says, "That at the name of Jesus every knee should bow, in heaven and on earth and under the earth, and every tongue acknowledge that Jesus Christ is Lord, to the glory of God the Father."

Father God, I come before Your throne boldly proclaiming that You are the great, I am, the author and the finisher of my faith. I ask that You continue to put me on the potter's wheel, molding and making me into the child of God that You would have me to be. As You work through me, give me a heart and mind to be a humble vessel, yielding to Your voice so that I can be empowered to walk in Your divine intent for life.

To my Alpha and Omega, I know without a doubt that we are approaching the end of times, You promised in Your Word that You will be coming back for a church without spots or wrinkles. When You return, You will be recognizable because on Your robe and Your thigh, it will be written that You are the King of kings and Lord of lords (Rev. 16:16, ESV). I am grateful that when You come back for me, I will live with You in paradise and reign with You for all eternity.

Entry Three

The Word of God tells us, "Declaring the end from the beginning, and from ancient times the things that are not yet done, saying, My counsel shall stand, and I will do all my pleasure" (Isa. 46:10, KJV).

Your Word is truth and will not return unto me void. I take heed to Your Word and humbly position myself to walk in the path of righteousness for Your name's sake. You are an awesome God with no restrictions on time because Your presence speaks eternity. You are the maker and controller of time here on Earth with a divine plan for the beginning and end of our lives. I am grateful that Your Word provides us with the instructions we need to conduct ourselves while we are yet here on earth.

I pledge to continue to live and work for Jesus, live in the spirit of expectation, knowing that You are coming back. Thank You so much for instructing me on how to discern false prophets that look and sound like the real deal but their mouths are far from the truth. Your Word tells me to watch out, and be on guard at all times, putting on the whole armor of God that shields me from the wiles of Satan's attacks. Overflowing with gratitude, I look forward to the coming of the rapture when I along with other believers, both in life and death, will meet our Lord and Savior in the clouds. What a glorious day it will be.

"And he said to me, 'It is done! I am the Alpha and the Omega, the beginning and the end. To the thirsty I will give from the spring of the water of life without payment.'" Revelation 21:6 (ESV)

Day 29

Wednesday, September 29, 2021

Jehovah-Hashopet: The Lord, Our Judge

Entry One

Our world is governed by a set of laws, rules, and boundaries that are designed to keep us safe and promote an orderly environment. When we break those rules, we can't help but think about the courtroom, judges, and jails. Consequently, when we think about God, we immediately think about heaven, which shifts our thoughts to hell. Make no mistake about it, there is a heaven and hell that is prepared for those of us that are obedient to the Word of God as well as those who are disobedient.

There is also a heavenly judge by the name of Jehovah-Hashopet, the Lord, our judge. He is the ultimate judge of all judges for none compares to His superlative and magnificent name. The Word of God has given us a defined set of instructions to govern ourselves while we reside on this earth. His standard of living supersedes the standards of the world, and His hand of judgment is consistent, just, and fair to all.

In the book of Revelation, God tells us, "The one who conquers and who keeps my works until the end, to him I will give authority over the nations, and he will rule them with a rod of iron, as when earthen pots are broken in pieces, even as I myself have received authority from my Father" (Rev. 2:26-27, ESV).

Jehovah-Hashopet, I am grateful that I serve a God who is just in all things, who commends and rewards me when I am obedient to His instructions of godly living. I can walk into eternity knowing that my Savior waits for me with His welcoming Words. Well done, my good and faithful servant. Can you imagine living and ruling with God for all eternity as one of the many rewards for being faithful over a few things? Thank You, Jesus.

Entry Two

I find it disheartening to say that we live in a society where equality is not equal. The justice system is corrupt with partial and impartial judgment for some who have committed the same crime. I have witnessed firsthand where one man goes to jail for years for distribution of drugs, while the other man, because of his status in the world, gets probation for the same crime.

Jehovah-Hashopet, I am so grateful that You are Lord over my life and judge my works according to Your divine standards. Thank You so much for showing mankind what justice and fairness should look like. Even when I'm wronged on this side of the earth, I fret not because You will be the final judge in the end that will judge the righteous and unrighteous. No one will escape your verdict for life or death.

God said in Acts 17:31 (ESV), "Because he has fixed a day on which he will judge the world in righteousness by a man whom he has appointed; and of this he has given assurance to all by raising him from the dead."

In addition, I'm reminded in 2 Peter of how God shows that He has no respect for a person when it comes to being just in all things. If God didn't spare even the angels when they sinned, casting them in a dark hell, chained and bound, what do You think about us? We often think of God as loving, compassionate, kind, and full of grace and mercy. This is accurate, but He is also a God of judgment. He said it in His Word and has no hidden agenda about the many names He holds as well as the guidelines for living a life that is committed to serving Him.

When we make a conscious choice to walk out of the safety net of God, we are outwardly choosing a life of the world that can lead us to destruction. God tells us that He came to the world to give us abundant life, not to kill or destroy us. He is pleading with us daily to repent of our sins and turn to Him for salvation so that we will receive a crown of life and many other gifts for our faithfulness on Earth.

Flooding with gratitude, I thank You for reminding me that the wages of sin is death, but You gave me life through confession, repentance, and acceptance of Jesus Christ as my Lord. I can go before the bar of judgment and face Jehovah-Hashopet because I will have Jesus by my side. Hallelujah!

Entry Three

The end of time is drawing near, and Jehovah-Hashopet is pleading for us to seek Him now while He can be found. God tells us that if we turn away from our wicked ways and turn to Him, He will have compassion on us and pardon our sins. When the Lord returns on the day of judgment, those that are in Christ will have no fear for this will be a day of rejoicing, but those who refuse to worship our Lord and Savior will be judged harshly, casting them into the burning fire.

God, I am grateful for Your living water that flows through my veins. As I walk before the bar of judgment, I walk with confidence because Jesus became my substitute in judgment, reaping no condemnation for me. On the day of judgment, anything that is corrupt or defiles itself against God will be destroyed. He's coming to create and new heaven and a new Earth, and He will not allow sin to enter into this new creation.

I am forever grateful to God when He said, "And if I go and prepare a place for you, I will come again, and receive you unto myself; that where I am, there ye may be also" (John 14:3, NIV).

Father God, I thank You for Jesus, and I look forward to this day as I will have a perfected body like that of Jesus Christ. I have faith in Your Word; Help me persevere to the end for I desire to receive a crown of life. You are the supreme judge, giver of life and death, infinite, eternal, all-sufficient, and all-powerful. Your name is to be exalted.

> *"Seek the Lord while he may be found; call upon him while he is near; let the wicked forsake his way, and the unrighteous man his thoughts; let him return to the Lord, that he may have compassion on him, and to our God, for he will abundantly pardon." Isaiah 55:6-7 (NIV)*

Day 30

Thursday, September 30, 2021

God is Omnipotent, Omniscient, And Omnipresent

Entry One

The countless names of God are an awe-inspiring revelation in my life. It is through each of His names that fill me with gratitude for His presence in my life. God is the Supreme Being of all things. He is limitless; a God that is all-powerful and all-mighty.

Psalm 147:4-5 (ESV) tells us, "He determines the number of the stars; he gives to all of them their names. Great is our Lord, and abundant in power; his understanding is beyond measure."

To my omnipotent God, while I know that You are all-sufficient and complete in Your work, I am honored to be Your servant, use me as a vessel to spread the gospel of salvation to all who will hear, listen, and be obedient to Your will and ways.

My mere thoughts of You inflate possibilities beyond anything that I can ever dream. Throughout my life, You have shown me that You can make the impossible a reality, bringing glory to Your name. Help me to remember that I don't have the capacity or resources to live an abundant life on my own; I need Your strength, Your footprints in the sand, carrying me.

Entry Two

Heavenly Father, I extol You with all my heart for You are a God who is perfectly loving and at the same time, perfectly just. When I think about the enormity of Your vastness and presence both in heaven and Earth, it blows my mind for the very thought of You is unfathomable. You occupy every space and crevice in the universe. You are omniscient, the all-knowing God who is aware of all things in the past, present, and future. There is nothing that escapes Your eye for every moment in the world plays like a movie before You, who is the director over the whole thing.

The Word of God declares, "For whenever our heart condemns us, God is greater than our heart, and he knows everything" (1 John 3:20, ESV).

I am indeed grateful that You know my heart, my condition, and the circumstances that surround me. Yet, in all Your knowings, You are gentle and loving, reminding me that You are bigger than my shortcomings could ever be. Thank You for seeing me, knowing my needs, and supplying me with Your blessings as You deliver me from the evils of this world. I am thrilled to be Your child, a God that knows and sees all; there is nothing that is missed by You from the beginning to the end. You are an amazing God.

Entry Three

I serve, glorify, and give praise to the great King who is above all gods; the One who creates all things. Your awesome presence transcends from the beginning to the end of times for You are present everywhere – the omnipresent God. I am amazed that while God is inside every space, he is also outside any space or dimension. Wow, that is mind-boggling for my finite mind. The Bible informs us that God's presence is so boundless that even the highest heaven cannot contain him.

"The eyes of the Lord are in every place, watching the evil and the good" (Prov. 15:3, NIV).

There is absolutely nothing that we can hide from God for he is all-seeing and all-knowing. We may be able to fool each other about who we are but God knows the very essence of us and the intent of our hearts. This reminds me of the movie To Tell The Truth, where a group of people claim to be the same person, and the panelist has to guess who the imposters are to identify the real person. The world operates under the same lens as we are professional actors on stage showing many faces in the span of our lives. However, in the spiritual world, we may as well come clean because there is no fooling God. He made us and He knows all about us.

Nevertheless, I find comfort in knowing that God is a loving and forgiving God who wants us to develop a relationship with him, holding back nothing. Thank You, heavenly Father, for Your presence in my life, watching over me, shielding me, "For we wrestle not against flesh and blood, but against principalities, against powers, against the rulers of the darkness of this world, against spiritual wickedness in high places" (Eph. 6:12, KJV).

I fear not because You are forever present, know all, and see all. I am safe and assured in knowing that I serve the Supreme Being of all things. Because of You, I am deemed more than a conqueror in Christ Jesus. When all others forsake me, I thank You, my Lord, for standing firm with me through the tests of time, holding my hand, coaching, and motivating me, giving me victory in the end. What a mighty God I serve.

"I am with you and will watch over you wherever you go, and I will bring you back to this land. I will not leave you until I have done what I have promised you." Genesis 28:15 (NIV)

Closing Thoughts

I give praise, honor, and glory to the Lord, the maker of heaven and Earth, for providing the opportunity for me to participate in the journey of gratitude. It has been a transformative experience and has shaped my attitude and outlook on life experiences. Exaltations unto God for releasing the Holy Spirit as my instructor to lead and guide me every step of the way. This gratitude experience became a reflective, purging, restoring, and cleansing process in my life.

I walk away with an increased sense of appreciation for who God is in my life, and all that He has done to bless my path from childhood to adulthood and into eternity. My experience with God during this thirty-day encounter of praise and gratitude unto Him has renewed and revitalized me spiritually. It was like a mist of dew that God poured out on me, bringing refreshment and productivity in my life, freeing me of insignificant tension that was designed to sap my energy. What a mighty God I serve.

Our heavenly Father deserves the best in all that we do. Each time I recorded an entry in my gratitude journal, God remained at the forefront of my mind. It was my reasonable service to work diligently and give up my best work and thoughts to show His glory and mighty hand in my life. Jehovah's desire for this book is to bless the body of Christ by distributing His Word to others through real and relevant encounters in this contemporary society.

It is my prayer and hope that this book will be an instrument to abundantly bless God's people. Even if it touches only one soul, the entire process will be more than gold. In short, we are called to bless God and serve and encourage one another. As a body of believers, let's cry out to God for transformation in our attitudes, restoring our joy, love, and appreciation of our blessings through the platform of gratitude.

I encourage you to take the first step in developing a gratitude journal of your own, releasing how grateful you are to God for blessing you daily. Each day you commit to going before God, exalting Him in all things; it will shift your attitude from negative thoughts to positive thoughts, finding God's blessing in the victories in Your life as well as the afflictions.

When we focus on a grateful heart, it brings us together in unity, giving us a heart and passion to render acts of kindness and serve each other with a pure heart. God wants you to enjoy your life here on Earth and experience a happy, fulfilled life. Count your blessings in all things and remember that you are still among the living while the lives of others have expired.

Christ is good news amid a dying world. When we change our attitude and outlook on life, we are empowered to change our circumstances. I continuously ask God to show me any hindrances in my life that separate me from Him. If He finds anything, I pray that He will fix it in the name of Jesus. If you have a heart that is willing and ready, God can transform you. In closing, I leave you with an inspired poem that was given to me under the unction of the Holy Spirit. Enjoy!

I Am So Grateful

By Dr. Rhonda A. Jaudon

Thank You, God, for Your awesome creation,

Thank You for heaven and thank You for the earth

The beauty of the ocean, stars, the entire universe!

Thank You for the moon.

Thank You for the sun.

Thank You for the rain and thank You for the pain.

Thank You for my ups

And thank You for my downs.

I give thanks to God for good times and when bad times lurks on my ground.

For I forge through the fire as You prepare me for something greater.

Thank You for being my redeemer, healer

Present help in a time of need

My Banner, Protector, Comforter

All-knowing, all-seeing, and forever present in my life.

You are God Almighty!

Thank You for Your mercy.

Thank You for Your Grace.

Thank You for Your love.

And Your gift of salvation, I will never waste.

I hold it dear to my heart with gratitude and praise.

I'm So Grateful!

CPSIA information can be obtained
at www.ICGtesting.com
Printed in the USA
BVHW041455220222
629771BV00014B/867